SUPERMAN
BY MARK MILLAR

SUPERMAN
BY MARK MILLAR

MARK MILLAR
writer

ALUIR AMANCIO · TERRY AUSTIN · GEORGES JEANTY
JACKSON GUICE · MIKE MANLEY · SEAN PHILLIPS
MIKE WIERINGO · DOUG HAZLEWOOD · RICHARD CASE
artists

MARIE SEVERIN
ROB SCHWAGER · LOVERN KINDZIERSKI
RICK TAYOR · PAMELA RAMBO · FELIX SERRANO
colorists

L. LOIS BUHALIS · PHILIP FELIX · BILL OAKLEY
COMICRAFT · TIM HARKINS · PAT PRENTICE
letterers

BRIAN STELFREEZE
collection cover artist

SUPERMAN created by JERRY SIEGEL and JOE SHUSTER
SUPERGIRL based on characters created by JERRY SIEGEL and JOE SHUSTER
SUPERBOY created by JERRY SIEGEL
By special arrangement with the Jerry Siegel family

MIKE McAVENNIE MAUREEN McTIGUE EDDIE BERGANZA JOEY CAVALIERI Editors – Original Series
FRANK BERRIOS Assistant Editor – Original Series
JEB WOODARD Group Editor – Collected Editions
ALEX GALER Editor – Collected Edition
STEVE COOK Design Director – Books
MEGEN BELLERSEN Publication Design

BOB HARRAS Senior VP – Editor-in-Chief, DC Comics
PAT McCALLUM Executive Editor, DC Comics

DIANE NELSON President
DAN DiDIO Publisher
JIM LEE Publisher
GEOFF JOHNS President & Chief Creative Officer
AMIT DESAI Executive VP – Business & Marketing Strategy, Direct to Consumer & Global Franchise Management
SAM ADES Senior VP & General Manager, Digital Services
BOBBIE CHASE VP & Executive Editor, Young Reader & Talent Development
MARK CHIARELLO Senior VP – Art, Design & Collected Editions
JOHN CUNNINGHAM Senior VP – Sales & Trade Marketing
ANNE DePIES Senior VP – Business Strategy, Finance & Administration
DON FALLETTI VP – Manufacturing Operations
LAWRENCE GANEM VP – Editorial Administration & Talent Relations
ALISON GILL Senior VP – Manufacturing & Operations
HANK KANALZ Senior VP – Editorial Strategy & Administration
JAY KOGAN VP – Legal Affairs
JACK MAHAN VP – Business Affairs
NICK J. NAPOLITANO VP – Manufacturing Administration
EDDIE SCANNELL VP – Consumer Marketing
COURTNEY SIMMONS Senior VP – Publicity & Communications
JIM (SKI) SOKOLOWSKI VP – Comic Book Specialty Sales & Trade Marketing
NANCY SPEARS VP – Mass, Book, Digital Sales & Trade Marketing
MICHELE R. WELLS VP – Content Strategy

SUPERMAN BY MARK MILLAR

Published by DC Comics. Compilation and all new material Copyright © 2018 DC Comics. All Rights Reserved. Originally published in single magazine form in SUPERMAN 80-PAGE GIANT 2, TEAM SUPERMAN 1, TANGENT COMICS: THE SUPERMAN 1, DC ONE MILLION 80-PAGE GIANT 1,000,000, SUPERMAN ADVENTURES 19, 25-27, 30, 31, 36, 52. Copyright © 1998, 1999, 2000 DC Comics. All Rights Reserved. All characters, their distinctive likenesses and related elements featured in this publication are trademarks of DC Comics. The stories, characters and incidents featured in this publication are entirely fictional. DC Comics does not read or accept unsolicited submissions of ideas, stories or artwork.

DC Comics, 2900 West Alameda Ave., Burbank, CA 91505
Printed by LSC Communications, Kendallville, IN, USA. 4/27/18. First Printing.
ISBN: 978-1-4012-7874-8

Library of Congress Cataloging-in-Publication Data is available.

TABLE OF CONTENTS

ALL STORIES WRITTEN BY MARK MILLAR

"LOIS, MY DEAR, SOMETHING HAPPENED TODAY THAT RESTORED MY FAITH IN HUMANITY. I BELIEVE I WITNESSED A MIRACLE WHERE THE FIRST NATIONAL BANK USED TO STAND.

"SUPERMAN, YOU MAY RECALL, DESTROYED THIS BUILDING DURING THE DOMINUS DEBACLE AND A CLEARLY TROUBLED MAN OF STEEL RETURNED THIS AFTERNOON TO OFFER HIS APOLOGIES.

"I MUST ADMIT, HE'S A POLISHED PERFORMER.

"HE SPOKE CLEARLY AND FROM THE HEART ABOUT HIS RECENT SHORTCOMINGS AND TOLD EVERYONE THAT HIS POWERS WERE ONCE AGAIN AT OUR DISPOSAL.

"HE EVEN OFFERED TO REBUILD THE BANK, ASSURING THE WORKERS THEY WOULD BE PAID IN FULL FOR HIS LABORS...

...BUT TO MY ASTONISHED DELIGHT, THEY REFUSED.

"THOSE FINE, UPSTANDING CITIZENS TOLD THAT PATRONIZING, ALIEN TRASH THAT THEY WERE MORE THAN CAPABLE OF LOOKING AFTER THEIR OWN AFFAIRS."

THE EXPRESSION OF DISAPPOINTMENT ON SUPERMAN'S FACE WAS THE MOST PERFECTLY BEAUTIFUL THING I HAVE *EVER* SEEN, LOIS.

IT'S AN IMAGE I PLAN TO COMMISSION IN OILS AND HANG ABOVE MY DESK FOR INSPIRATION.

SAVE THE MELODRAMATIC SPEECH FOR THE INTERNS, LEX, I HEARD ALL YOUR BEST LINES YEARS AGO.

PERSONALLY, I'M MORE INTERESTED IN WHY YOU THINK THOSE CONSTRUCTION WORKERS TURNED DOWN SUPERMAN'S KIND OFFER.

ANY THEORIES OF THE *NON-LUNATIC* VARIETY?

THE PUBLIC SIMPLY DOESN'T TRUST HIM ANYMORE, DEAR GIRL.

MY LONG-STANDING BELIEF THAT HE IS A DANGER TO SOCIETY IS NO LONGER AN ISOLATED OPINION, ACCORDING TO OUR COMPETITORS IN THE PRINT MEDIA.

METROPOLIS EAGLE

GET OUT OF METROPOLIS SUPERMAN

LET'S SEE HOW FAST HIS *SAMARITAN* FACADE *DISAPPEARS* WHEN THE CHEERING STOPS AND THEY PULL DOWN HIS PREPOSTEROUS STATUES.

WHAT? ARE YOU SERIOUSLY SUGGESTING THE ONLY REASON SUPER-MAN DEVOTES HIS LIFE TO HELPING PEOPLE IS BECAUSE HE SOAKS UP THE ADULATION?

NATURALLY, LOIS...

...UNLESS, OF COURSE, YOU SUSPECT THE TRUE MOTIVE BEHIND HIS ACTIONS IS OF A MORE *SINISTER* VARIETY?

8

LEX LUTHOR IS AN INTELLECTUAL WHIRLWIND. THESE OCCASIONAL LUNCHTIME BRAINSTORMING SESSIONS MAKE WORKING FOR LEXCOM *ALMOST* STIMULATING SOMETIMES...

...BUT, IQ OF 240 OR NOT, HE'LL NEVER UNDERSTAND WHAT MAKES MY HUSBAND TICK IN A HUNDRED MILLION YEARS.

CLARK DOESN'T CARE ABOUT PARADES OR APPLAUSE. HE ONLY ADOPTED THE SUPERMAN IDENTITY BECAUSE I FORCED HIS HAND, AND THE COSTUME AND CAPE WERE HIS MOM'S IDEA.

HE WAS PERFECTLY HAPPY HELPING PEOPLE IN SECRET UNTIL I MADE HIM INTO A RELUCTANT CELEBRITY.

WITH OR WITHOUT HIS GLASSES, HE'S THE MOST SENSITIVE MAN I'VE EVER KNOWN. IT KILLS ME TO HEAR THE PUBLIC MOAN ABOUT HIM WHEN I KNOW HE'S LISTENING TO EVERY WORD.

I CAN APPRECIATE PEOPLE ARE SCARED AFTER THE TERRIBLE THINGS DOMINUS MADE HIM DO, BUT IF ONLY THEY HAD AN INKLING HOW MANY TIMES HE WOULD DIE FOR EACH AND EVERY ONE OF THEM.

THEY COULDN'T POSSIBLY BE *AFRAID* OF MY SUPERMAN IF THEY KNEW WHAT HE WAS *REALLY* LIKE.

THE WORLD CAN ONLY SEE A STAINLESS MAN OF STEEL WRAPPED IN THE STARS AND STRIPES, BUT THE TRUTH IS THAT HE'S AS INSECURE AS THE REST OF US UNDERNEATH THAT THICK, IMPENETRABLE SKIN.

MOST SIGNIFICANT OF ALL IS HIS FEAR OF BEING ALONE...

BIOLOGY SUGGESTS THAT I'LL DIE LONG BEFORE HE DOES AND, IN HIS QUIETEST MOMENTS, HE ADMITS THIS CHILLS HIM TO THE MARROW.

OCCASIONALLY, WHEN I'M STRESSED OR EATING TOO MUCH JUNK, I THINK I FEEL THE MILD TINGLE OF HIS X-RAYS AS HE SCANS MY ARTERIES OR CHECKS MY CHOLESTEROL, ALTHOUGH I KNOW BETTER.

RIGHT NOW HE'S GOT ME ON SOME KIND OF MACROBIOTIC DIET UTILIZING PLANTS AND MINERALS ONLY FOUND ON THE PACIFIC RIM.

PERSONALLY, I DON'T CARE WHAT I EAT SO LONG AS SOMEONE ELSE DOES THE COOKING WHICH, I'M DELIGHTED TO SAY, HE RELISHES AS MUCH AS HE ENJOYS THE REST OF THE HOUSEWORK.

HE BARELY NEEDS TO SLEEP AT ALL, BUT HOLDS ME IN HIS ARMS EVERY NIGHT UNTIL THE DAWN BREAKS ANYWAY. NOT A SINGLE DAY BEGINS WHERE HE DOESN'T TELL ME HOW MUCH HE LOVES ME.

NOT A SINGLE NIGHT DRAWS TO A CLOSE WHERE HE DOESN'T SAY HOW LUCKY HE WAS TO FIND LOIS JOANNE LANE.

IF I'M HONEST WITH MYSELF, I'LL ADMIT I WASN'T A VERY NICE PERSON BEFORE HE CAME ALONG AND PROVED IT WAS POSSIBLE TO BE INFATUATED WITH SOMETHING OUTSIDE OF MY CAREER.

I'D ALWAYS DATED RICH, POWERFUL MEN, BUT EVEN THE BEST OF THEM SEEMED MORE LIKE RIVALS AND ALL I WAS REALLY INTERESTED IN WAS PROVING I WAS SMARTER THAN THEY WERE, ANYWAY.

SUPERMAN NEVER PROVOKED THAT KIND OF TOMBOY BEHAVIOR.

THIS WAS MY FIRST GENUINELY ADULT RELATIONSHIP, BASED ON THE ALTOGETHER ALIEN CONCEPT OF MUTUAL RESPECT.

YOU MIGHT THINK A CHILDHOOD SQUANDERED IN ARMY BASES AND A MOSTLY-ABSENT DAD MIGHT MEAN I WAS LOOKING FOR AN ALL-PROTECTING FATHER-FIGURE, BUT YOU COULDN'T BE MORE WRONG.

I DIDN'T SEE A SUPERHERO AS THE PATRIARCHAL ANSWER TO ALL MY PROBLEMS, AS SOME FEMINIST AUTHORS MIGHT SUGGEST...

...I JUST FINALLY FOUND A MAN WHO COULD KEEP UP WITH ME.

HIS PLAYFULNESS, HIS CLUBHOUSE IN THE SNOW AND ALL THE LITTLE CURIOSITIES HE KEEPS LOCKED UP INSIDE INDICATE TO ME THAT HERE IS SOMEONE WHO HAS NEVER LOST HIS ENTHUSIASM FOR LIFE.

HE COMBINES THE BEST THINGS ABOUT BEING A CHILD WITH THE ESSENTIAL QUALITIES OF A MAN AND THIS, IN MY OPINION, ARE THE INGREDIENTS OF A SUPERMAN.

I JUST WISH THAT, AS A WRITER, I COULD FIND THE WORDS TO MAKE THEM TRUST HIM AGAIN. DEAL THE LITTLE THINGS THAT MADE ME FALL IN LOVE WITH HIM WITHOUT ENDANGERING THE SECRET...

...LIKE HIS FAVORITE BOOKS, OR FOOD, THE UTTERLY *BIZARRE* THINGS THAT MAKE HIM LAUGH.

THE FACT THAT A TOUGH, PULITZER PRIZE-WINNING REPORTER WITH A PUSHY, VOLATILE PERSONALITY IS SO PROUD OF WHAT HE DOES THAT SHE ACTUALLY *INSISTS* ON IRONING HIS UNIFORMS.

HE'S SUCH A SPECIAL PERSON...

...THERE MUST BE SOMETHING I CAN SAY TO REMIND PEOPLE.

CALL 911! WE GOT A FIRE DOWN THE STREET!

A FIRE?!

12

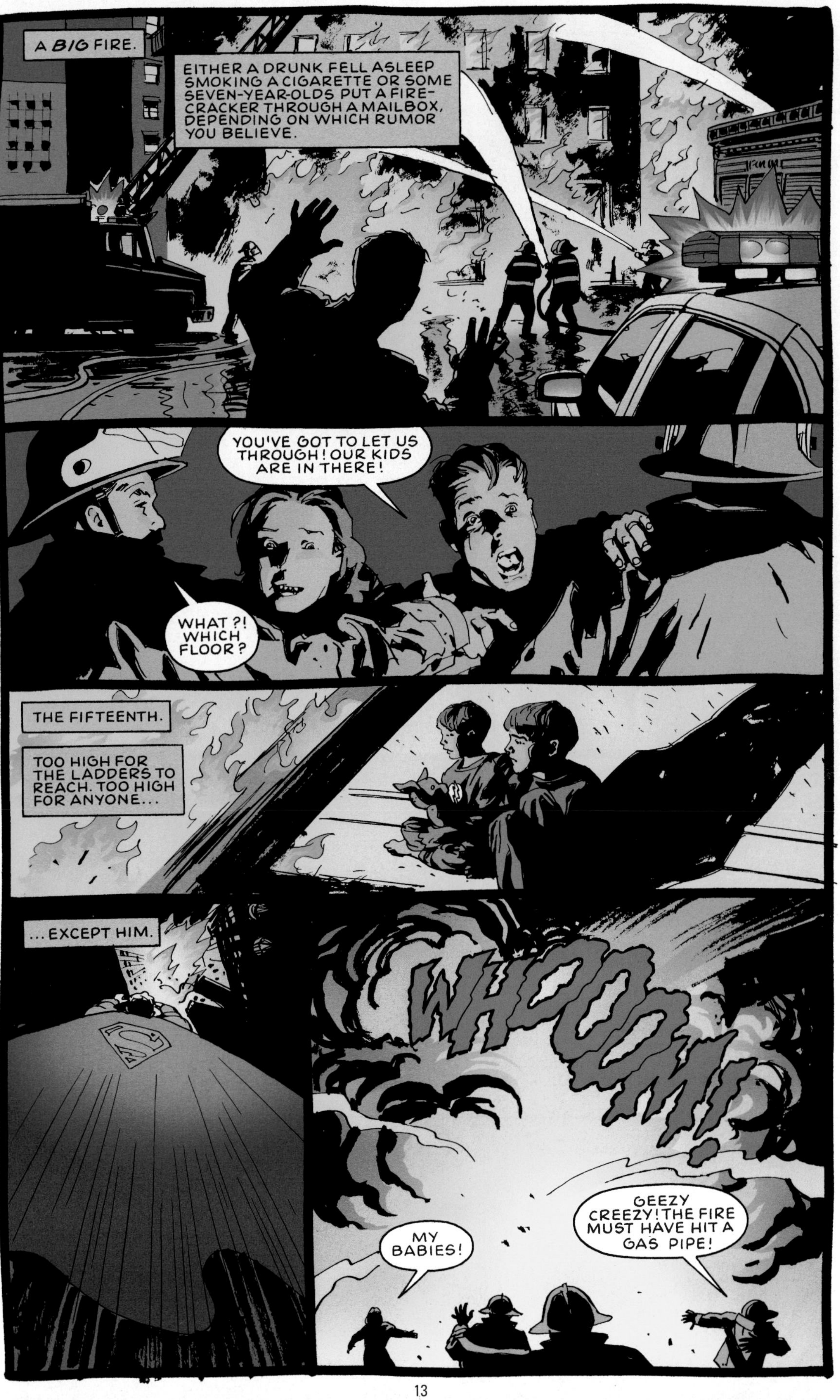
A *BIG* FIRE.
EITHER A DRUNK FELL ASLEEP SMOKING A CIGARETTE OR SOME SEVEN-YEAR-OLDS PUT A FIRE-CRACKER THROUGH A MAILBOX, DEPENDING ON WHICH RUMOR YOU BELIEVE.
YOU'VE GOT TO LET US THROUGH! OUR KIDS ARE IN THERE!
WHAT?! WHICH FLOOR?
THE FIFTEENTH.
TOO HIGH FOR THE LADDERS TO REACH. TOO HIGH FOR ANYONE...
...EXCEPT HIM.
WHOOOM!
MY BABIES!
GEEZY CREEZY! THE FIRE MUST HAVE HIT A GAS PIPE!

PRESENT AND ACCOUNTED FOR, MA'AM.

LOOK! UP IN THE SKY...!

DON'T SCARE MOMMY LIKE THAT! DON'T EVER SCARE MOMMY LIKE THAT AGAIN, YOU HEAR?

BUT YOU DON'T UNDERSTAND... MINDY'S STILL IN THERE! YOU'VE GOT TO GO BACK AND SAVE HER OR SHE'LL DIE!

THIS IS JUST VINTAGE SUPERMAN. IF THESE PEOPLE HAD SEEN THIS BEFORE ALL THE RECENT PROBLEMS, IT WOULD HAVE TAKEN A FIRE HOSE TO CALM THEM DOWN.

TAKE IT EASY, HONEY. MINDY'S FINE.

AS IT IS, THEY'VE READ SO MUCH GARBAGE ABOUT HIM THAT THEY DON'T KNOW HOW TO REACT...

...EVEN WHEN THEY SEE HIM DO SOMETHING MAGNIFICENT.

IT'S SO UNFAIR I WANT TO CRY.

SUPERMAN

WUSS

I JUST CAN'T STAND HERE AND LET THIS GO UNNOTICED.

LET ME THROUGH... WHAT'S THE MATTER WITH YOU PEOPLE? ISN'T A MAN ALLOWED TO MAKE ONE MISTAKE?!!

WAY TO GO, SUPERMAN!

DAMN STRAIGHT. DID YOU SEE THE WAY HE SWOOPED OUTTA THAT BUILDING? I THOUGHT THOSE KIDS WERE DEAD FOR SURE.

THANK YOU, SUPERMAN. THANK YOU SO MUCH.

YOU SAID IT THAT MAN'S A MIRACLE.

HE'S ALWAYS TOO BUSY THINKING ABOUT THE REST OF US TO CARE WHAT PEOPLE ARE SAYING ABOUT HIM...

...BUT I CARE.

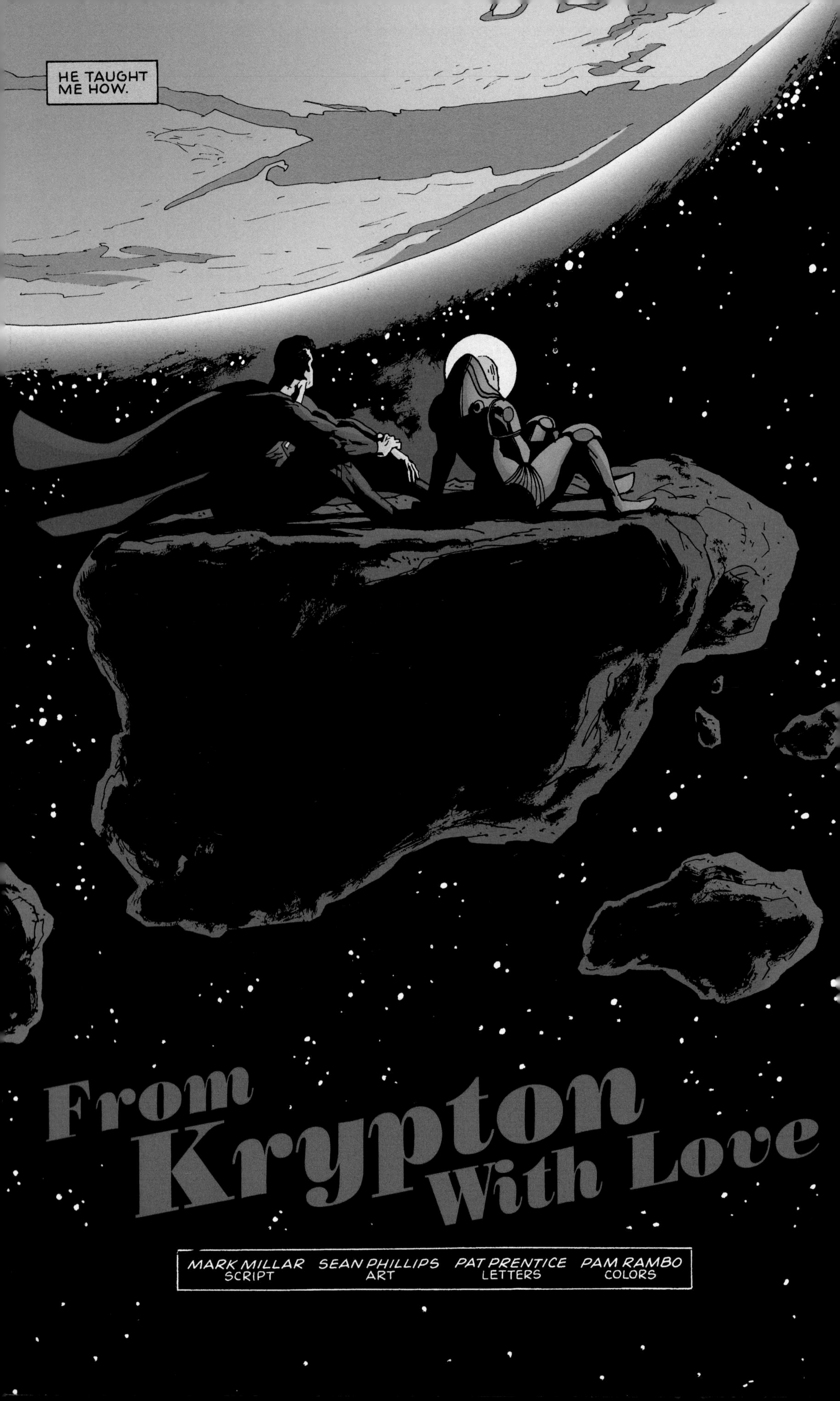
HE TAUGHT ME HOW.
From Krypton With Love
MARK MILLAR SCRIPT
SEAN PHILLIPS ART
PAT PRENTICE LETTERS
PAM RAMBO COLORS

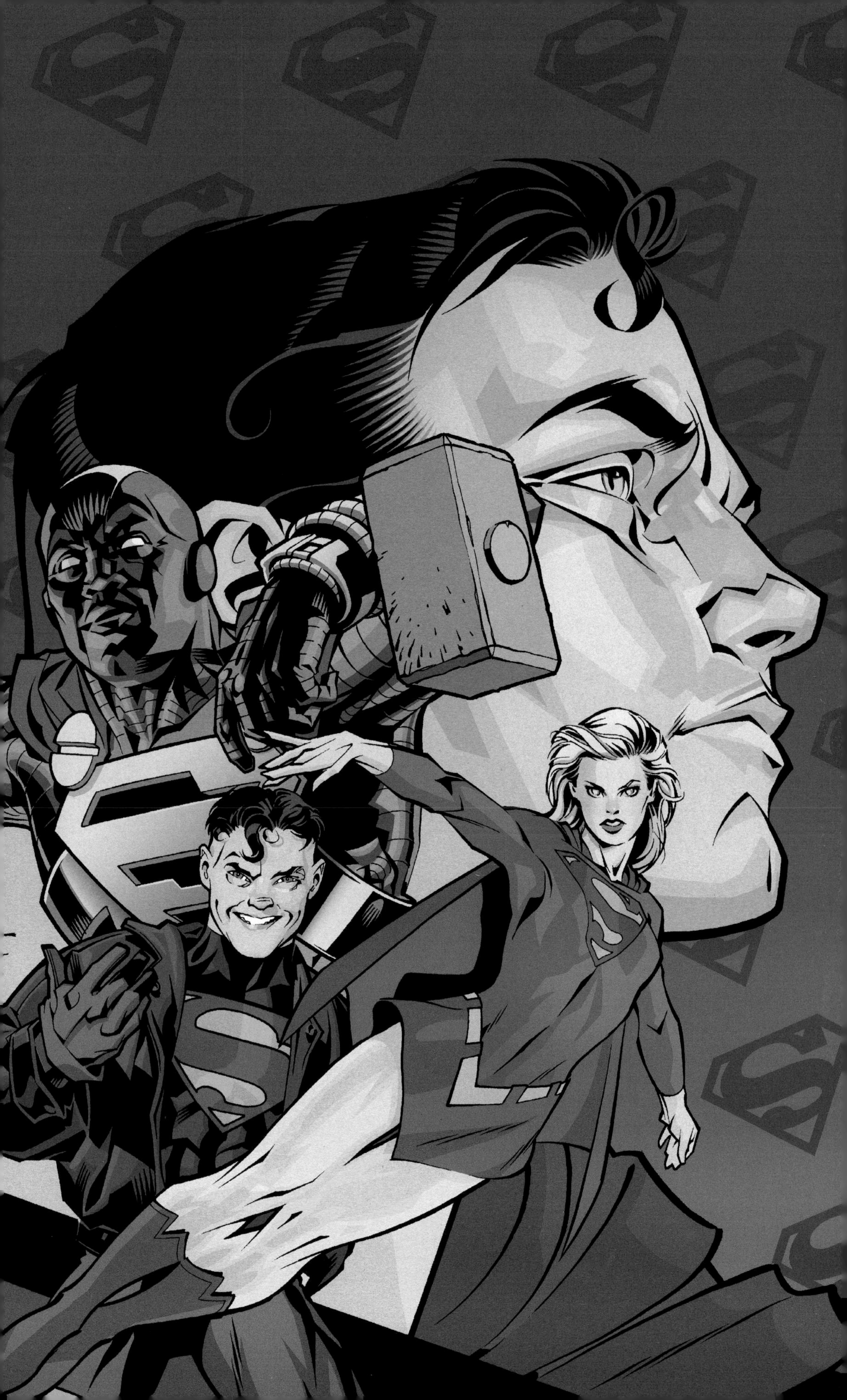

HELLO?

THEY DIED WITH THEIR CAPES ON

MARK MILLAR   GEORGES JEANTY   DOUG HAZLEWOOD
writer   penciller   inker
BILL OAKLEY   ROB SCHWAGER   MAUREEN McTIGUE
letterer   color & seps   editor

Cover by BRIAN STELFREEZE

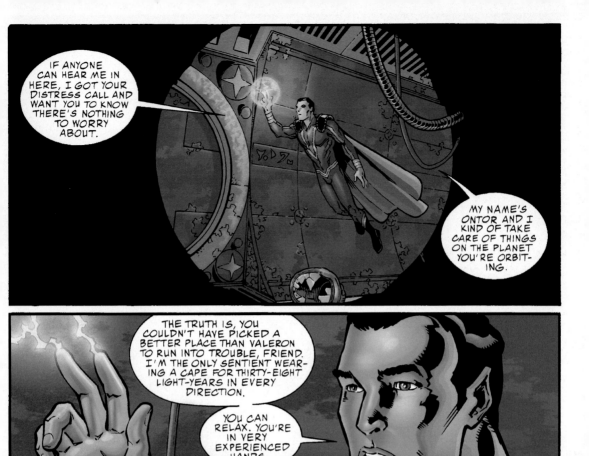

IF ANYONE CAN HEAR ME IN HERE, I GOT YOUR DISTRESS CALL AND WANT YOU TO KNOW THERE'S NOTHING TO WORRY ABOUT.

MY NAME'S ONTOR AND I KIND OF TAKE CARE OF THINGS ON THE PLANET YOU'RE ORBITING.

THE TRUTH IS, YOU COULDN'T HAVE PICKED A BETTER PLACE THAN VALERON TO RUN INTO TROUBLE, FRIEND. I'M THE ONLY SENTIENT WEARING A CAPE FOR THIRTY-EIGHT LIGHT-YEARS IN EVERY DIRECTION.

YOU CAN RELAX. YOU'RE IN VERY EXPERIENCED HANDS.

AAAUUUUHHHH!

MERCIFUL GODS!

THAT'S THE WAY. BIG, DEEP BREATHS...

THIS LITTLE OXYGEN AURA I'VE GENERATED SHOULD KEEP YOU COMFORTABLE UNTIL WE CAN GET OUR PICO-MACHINES TO LOOK AT YOU AND REPAIR ANY INTERNAL DAMAGE YOU'VE SUSTAINED.

NOW PLEASE, SIR, THIS IS VERY IMPORTANT. ARE THERE ANY OTHER PEOPLE ON BOARD THIS SHIP WHO COULD USE SOME HELP?

NONE WHATSOEVER.

EEEEIIIGHH!

COMPUTER, RESUME VOICE-CONTROL.

ACTIVATE CLOAK.

W-WHO ARE YOU? WHAT DID YOU PUT IN MY HEAD?

JUST A NEURO-LOGICAL COMMAND I STOLE FROM A TELEPATHIC SUPER-HERO IN ALPHA CEN-TAURI. HE WAS A CON-FIRMED PACIFIST WHO SUBDUED HIS ENEMIES--

--WITHOUT EVER RAISING HIS HAND IN ANGER.

THEY SAY I WAS THE FIRST HE EVER TOOK A SWING AT.

I KEPT HIS FIST AS A SOUVENIR.

YOU CAN CALL ME THE ANTI-HERO, INCIDENTALLY.

THE TWO OF US ARE GOING TO BE SPENDING A GREAT DEAL OF TIME TO-GETHER FOR THE TIME BEING.

WHAT IS THIS PLACE?

YOU REALIZE I CAN BE OUT OF HERE IN TEN SECONDS?

NO, YOU CAN'T.

MY WORKSHOP. THIS IS WHERE I TORTURE AND KILL SUPER-HEROES. I'VE BEEN DISSECTING AND STEALING POWERS FROM YOU BRIGHT-EYED IMBECILES SINCE THE UNIVERSE WAS HALF ITS PRESENT SIZE.

EVEN IF YOU COULD, I'D ONLY PUT YOU BACK INSIDE. EVERY SUPER-POWER I'VE EVER STOLEN CAN BE ACCESSED FROM MY MAINFRAME COMPUTER. I'M STRONG, SMART, COSMICALLY-AWARE...

ONLY THE BEST, ONLY THE MOST-REVERED, WILL DO.

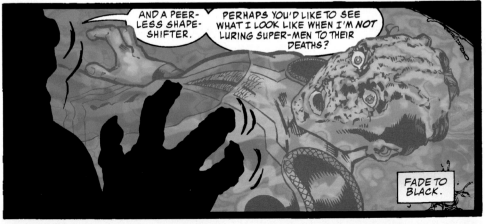

AND A PEER-LESS SHAPE-SHIFTER.

PERHAPS YOU'D LIKE TO SEE WHAT I LOOK LIKE WHEN I'M NOT LURING SUPER-MEN TO THEIR DEATHS?

FADE TO BLACK.

METROPOLIS AIRPORT.

GOOD THING CLARK *DIDN'T* JOIN US THIS MORNING, LOIS. THAT FLU HE'S BEEN TRYING TO SHAKE OFF WOULD HAVE TURNED INTO *PNEUMONIA* STANDING AROUND IN THIS WEATHER.

WHO ARE THESE NUT JOBS ANYWAY, JIMMY? I ONLY ENJOY WAITING FOR TERRORISTS I'VE ACTUALLY *HEARD* OF WHEN IT'S THIS COLD.

SOME KIND OF RIGHT-WING EXTREMISTS, ACCORDING TO THE FEDS. BORROWED THEIR CODE NAMES FROM IMPRESSIONIST ARTISTS: RENOIR, MONET, DEGAS, TOULOUSE-LAUTREC...

A TERRORIST WHO CALLS HIMSELF TOULOUSE-LAUTREC?

SECRETARY OF STATE HAS BEEN CONFIRMED AS A PASSENGER.

THAT'S RIGHT, BOYS YOU HEARD ME *CORRECTLY*...

...POWER MUST BE TAKEN AWAY FROM THE MYSTERY MEN ON THE MOON--

--AND GIVEN BACK TO THE AMERICAN PEOPLE.

THE DRAFT-DODGER EITHER OUTLAWS ALL META-HUMAN ACTIVITY IN THE UNITED STATES FROM MIDNIGHT TONIGHT, OR MY GROUP AND I START DECORATING THE AIRCRAFT IN A BRAND-NEW SHADE OF RED!

LADIES AND GENTLEMEN, IF YOU'D ALL FASTEN YOUR SAFETY BELTS, THIS FLIGHT WILL ARRIVE AT METROPOLIS AIRPORT IN TEN MINUTES AS SCHEDULED. EVERYBODY TAKE IT EASY...

...EXCEPT YOU, MADAME SECRETARY. YOU'RE BAILING OUT WITH US.

DEPENDS ON HOW MUCH YOU CARE FOR BEING THREE-DIMENSIONAL, HONEY.

YOU'RE NOT SUGGESTING I WEAR A PARACHUTE...?

THE SECOND THIS AIRCRAFT REACHES A SAFE HEIGHT, WE'RE JUMPING OUT WITH THE ONLY HOSTAGE THAT MATTERS... PARACHUTE OR *NOT*.

THIS MISSION IS NOT TURNING INTO ONE OF THOSE AIRPORT SIEGES WHERE MY BOYS AND I GET OUR BRAINS BLOWN OUT BY THE PRESIDENT'S NEW WORLD ORDER STORM TROOPERS.

DEGAS, WE'VE GOT COMPANY!

WHAT? BUT WE'RE NOT EVEN IN *METROPOLIS* YET!

TRY TELLING THAT TO *HIM*.

IF YOU'RE LISTENING, SUPERMAN, IT'S SPEEDING BULLET TIME.

STEP OUTSIDE AND WE'LL TALK ABOUT IT.

HHRUNCH

THE QUESTION IS: CAN YOU MOVE FAST ENOUGH TO KEEP OUR CAUSE OUT OF THE HEADLINES? ANSWERS ON A POSTCARD...

AAAAAA

DEGAAAS!

THANK YOU FOR FLYING LEX-AIR, GENTLEMEN.

I HOPE YOU HAD A PLEASANT JOURNEY.

KLIK

RENOIR WHAT'S WRONG WITH MONET?

JUST TRYING TO PUT SOME DISTANCE BETWEEN ME AND PLAN B IN THE CARGO HOLD.

WHY ISN'T HE OPENING HIS CHUTE?

IT'S A BOMB...

BOOM

"FOUR HUNDRED AND TWENTY-SEVEN PEOPLE ARE NO LONGER LIVING AND BREATHING TODAY, INCLUDING THE U.S. SECRETARY OF STATE AND HER FAMILY, BECAUSE OF MY CARELESSNESS..."

FOUR HUNDRED AND TWENTY-SEVEN LIVES ENDED ABRUPTLY LAST NIGHT BECAUSE I USED MY POWERS WITHOUT THINKING ABOUT THE CONSEQUENCES.

WHEN I PUT ON THIS COSTUME, I DID SO TO PRESERVE HUMAN LIFE, AND PROTECT YOU FROM THE NEW KINDS OF THREATS WHICH WERE EMERGING IN A RAPIDLY CHANGING WORLD.

LAST NIGHT, MY INCOMPETENCE PROVED BEYOND ALL REASONABLE DOUBT THAT THE CRITICS OF THE SUPER-HUMAN EFFORT HAVE SOME MORAL JUSTIFICATION.

I'VE LIVED AMONG YOU FOR SOME TIME, MADE THE BEST FRIENDS A MAN COULD HAVE, LOVED YOU MORE THAN YOU COULD EVER UNDERSTAND. AND THIS MAKES WHAT I HAVE TO SAY VERY DIFFICULT...

SECRETARY-GENERAL, LADIES AND GENTLEMEN, I WISH TO DECLARE MY INTENTIONS TO CEASE MY RESPONSIBILITIES AND LEAVE THIS PLANET IMMEDIATELY.

IN WHAT CAN ONLY BE DESCRIBED AS A BOMBSHELL WHICH HAS ROCKED METROPOLIS **AND THE WORLD...**

SHOCK RESIGNATION...

SUPERMAN LEFT THE U.N. BUILDING GIVING NO CLUES WHERE HE WAS HEADING, ALTHOUGH SPECULATION HAS RANGED FROM A RUMORED RETREAT IN THE ARCTIC TO THE RED STAR WORLD OF DAXAM...

BLAMING HIMSELF FOR THE DEATH OF EVERYONE ON BOARD...

SUPERGIRL WAS THE FIRST TO PLEDGE HER SUPPORT TO THE NERVOUS CITIZENS OF METROPOLIS AFTER AN APPEAL FROM THE PRESIDENT TO THE SUPERHUMAN COMMUNITY FOR TEMPORARY PROTECTION...

BOTH GREEN LANTERN AND THE FLASH ARE SAID TO BE CONSIDERING ASSISTANCE POSITIONS...

SUPERBOY OFFERED HIS SERVICES SHORTLY AFTERWARDS, RAISING HOPES THAT SOME NEW KIND OF ALLIANCE WAS FORMING TO WATCH OVER THE BIG APRICOT IN THE WAKE OF SUPERMAN'S DEPARTURE.

STEEL HAS SO FAR BEEN UNAVAILABLE FOR COMMENT.

WHERE HAS SUPERMAN GONE?

NUMEROUS SIGHTINGS, BUT NOTHING SUBSTANTIATED.

PEOPLE ARE DESPERATE TO SEE SOMEONE UP IN THE SKIES AGAIN.

SPARKING A STRING OF SUICIDES.

A MASS HYSTERIA UNSEEN SINCE HIS ENCOUNTER WITH DOOMSDAY.

DIRECTOR OF THE LEXCORP GROUP EXPRESSED DEEP SADNESS.

STEEL'S TAKING THIS BADLY. HE'S JUST BEEN SITTING IN THE MONITOR WOMB FOR HOURS, WATCHING BROADCAST AFTER BROADCAST.

JOHN IRONS WAS INFLUENCED BY SUPERMAN MORE THAN ANY OF US, FLASH. HE EVEN WEARS THE SYMBOL ON HIS CHEST AS A MARK OF RESPECT. HIS REACTION IS HARDLY SURPRISING.

WHAT ABOUT YOU, J'ONN? DON'T YOU THINK IT SEEMS A LITTLE OUT OF CHARACTER FOR SUPERMAN TO JUST *QUIT* LIKE THIS?

KAL-EL IS A MORE INTROSPECTIVE MAN THAN ANYONE WOULD CARE TO IMAGINE, WALLY. A TELEPATHIC SCAN UNCOVERED A LEVEL OF GUILT I CANNOT DESCRIBE IN ANY HUMAN LANGUAGE.

PRAYERS FOR HIS RETURN OFFERED BY THE POPE.

HE ASKED FOR PRIVACY AND I SUGGEST WE RESPECT THAT REQUEST.

WHEREVER HE IS RIGHT NOW, I ONLY HOPE HE HAS FOUND SOME RESPITE FROM THE SUFFERING HE'S ENDURED.

"WHEN I PUT ON THIS COSTUME, I DID SO TO PRESERVE HUMAN LIFE AND PROTECT YOU FROM THE NEW KINDS OF THREATS WHICH WERE EMERGING IN A RAPIDLY-CHANGING WORLD.

"LAST NIGHT, MY INCOMPETENCE PROVED BEYOND ALL REASONABLE DOUBT THAT THE CRITICS OF THE SUPERHUMAN EFFORT HAVE SOME MORAL JUSTIFICATION.

"I'VE LIVED AMONG YOU FOR SOME TIME, MADE THE BEST FRIENDS A MAN COULD HAVE, LOVED YOU MORE THAN YOU COULD EVER UNDERSTAND. AND THIS MAKES WHAT I HAVE TO SAY VERY DIFFICULT...

"SECRETARY-GENERAL, LADIES AND GENTLEMEN, I WISH TO DECLARE MY INTENTION TO CEASE MY RESPONSIBILITIES AND LEAVE THIS PLANET IMMEDIATELY."

SOUND CONVINCING?

TO BE HONEST, I THOUGHT THE MARTIAN MIND-SCAN WOULD BE MORE OF A PROBLEM, BUT J'ONN J'ONZZ IS ONLY A FEW THOUSAND YEARS OLD AND STILL TRUSTS WHAT HE HEARS IN HIS HEAD.

EVERYONE ELSE WAS SO DISTRACTED BY THE SCENARIO I DEVISED, THE QUESTION OF WHETHER I WAS THE GENUINE ARTICLE OR NOT WAS NEVER EVEN RAISED.

EVERY ANGLE HAS BEEN COVERED. THE PERFECT CRIME HAS BEEN COMMITTED. EARTH'S BRIGHTEST STAR HAS BEEN CAPTURED, AND NONE OF HIS *IDIOTIC* ALLIES ARE EVEN LOOKING FOR HIM.

THE ANTI-HERO WINS AGAIN. JUST LIKE ALWAYS.

OH, SUPERMAN, EVEN A MAN OF STEEL MUST TURN TO *JELLY* WHEN HE LOOKS UPON THESE SYMBOLS ON MY WALL AND REALIZES HIS OWN IS *SURE* TO HANG BESIDE THEM SOON ENOUGH.

HOW HUMILIATING IS IT TO KNOW THAT THE ONLY THING KEEPING YOU ALIVE IS THE FACT THAT YOUR WHIMPERS STILL AMUSE ME?

I TRAINED MYSELF TO BE AN EXPERT IN ALL FORMS OF PAIN WITH A DETAILED KNOWLEDGE OF EVERY ALIEN PHYSIOLOGY IN EXISTENCE, BUT KRYPTONIAN WAS ALWAYS MY PARTICULAR *SPECIALTY.*

ISN'T THAT A HAPPY COINCIDENCE?

THE ANTI-HERO *CAPTURES,* THE ANTI-HERO *TORTURES...*

...THE ANTI-HERO ELIMINATES!

EEEAAAAAGGGH!

NO ONE CAN SEE THEM. NO ONE CAN HEAR THEM.

EVERY FACTOR THAT MIGHT ALERT THE OTHERS TO HIS WHEREABOUTS HAS BEEN CALCULATED TO THE TENTH DECIMAL POINT...

...THE POSSIBILITY OF RESCUE IS NONEXISTENT.

CLARK'S RESIGNATION WAS A *FAKE*, SUPERGIRL.

MY HUSBAND'S IN TROUBLE.

LOIS, HE'S A VERY UNUSUAL MAN. HE MIGHT HAVE REASONS FOR HIS DISAPPEARANCE YOU AND I COULD NEVER HOPE TO UNDERSTAND.

YOU HAVE TO REMEMBER SUPERMAN'S NOT EXACTLY *HUMAN.*

HE SHOOK MY HAND AND SAID GOODBYE TO ME WITH THE SAME LOVE AND REGRET IN HIS EYES HE HAD FOR JIMMY OLSEN.

DOESN'T THAT STRIKE YOU AS THE SLIGHTEST BIT SUSPICIOUS?

WHOEVER'S BEHIND THIS HAS OBVIOUSLY DONE HIS HOMEWORK, BUT HE'S MISSING ONE VITAL SCRAP OF INFORMATION ABOUT SUPERMAN THAT ISN'T PUBLIC KNOWLEDGE. AT LEAST, NOT *YET,* ANYWAY.

HE DIDN'T KNOW ABOUT THE *SECRET.*

CLARK DOESN'T WEAR A MASK. IT WAS AN EASY MISTAKE TO MAKE, BUT THAT DOESN'T MAKE MY SITUATION ANY LESS DIFFICULT. HOW CAN I HELP HIM WITHOUT TELLING THE WORLD SUPERMAN'S SECRET IDENTITY?

THIS IS EXACTLY THE KIND OF NIGHTMARE SITUATION HE USED TO WORRY ABOUT ALL THOSE YEARS WHEN HE KEPT ME IN THE DARK.

I'M GOING TO HAVE TO TELL THEM, SUPERGIRL. NO MATTER WHAT IT MEANS FOR ANY OF US. CLARK'S LIFE COULD BE AT STAKE, HERE AND THAT'S MORE IMPORTANT THAN THE SECRET EVER WAS.

I HAVE TO TELL THE WORLD THE TRUTH.

GIVE ME TWENTY-FOUR HOURS.

A TEAM IS PUT TOGETHER.

BATMAN SAID IT WAS *OBVIOUS* THIS SUPERMAN WAS AN IMPOSTOR AFTER HE EXAMINED THE RESIGNATION TAPES

APPARENTLY, THE SUPERMAN *WE* KNOW BLINKS TWENTY PERCENT MORE UNDER STRESS.

PLUS, THE SENTENCE STRUCTURE INCONSISTENCIES BETWEEN THE TWO WERE SO GLARING AN AMATEUR COULD SPOT THEM.

YEAH, RIGHT. *AFTER* WE TELL HIM. HOW OBSERVANT WAS THE MASTER DETECTIVE WHEN THE CREEP WAS KISSING THE JLA GOODBYE?

SUPERBOY, PLEASE. WE NEED A STRATEGY, NOT SOMEONE TO BLAME.

THE MOST TIME-EFFICIENT WAY OF FINDING SUPERMAN IS THE TWELVE JLA-LED TEAMS, COVERING ONE TWELFTH OF THE PLANET.

OUR CODE NAME IS TEAM SUPERMAN, BUT WE'LL BE IN CONSTANT LINK WITH THE OTHERS, IN CASE WE NEED REINFORCEMENTS.

HENCE THE HEADSETS. NOW LET'S STOP WASTING TIME.

THE HEADSETS ARE FOR COMMUNICATING WITH EACH OTHER, KID. LEAGUE MEMBERS HAVE AN ESTABLISHED TELEPATHIC LINK WITH THE MARTIAN MANHUNTER.

HE'S READING YOUR MIND, huh?

SKIES LOOK CLEAR FOR TAKE OFF GENTLEMEN.

BETTER NOT FLY BEHIND SUPERGIRL WHILE SHE'S WEARING THAT SKIRT.

WHAT COORDINATES ARE WE SUPPOSED TO BE COVERING, JOHN?

SWEEPING NORTH EIGHTY DEGREES LONGITUDE, FROM WEST EIGH- THROUGH EAST MERIDIA- TWENTY DEGREES LATITUDE.

OTHERWISE KNOWN AS THE ARCTIC CIRCLE.

SCIENTISTS HAVE SUCH A ROMANTIC WAY OF LOOKING AT THE WORLD, DON'T YOU THINK?

SUPERBOY, I REALIZE MAKING IRRITATING JOKES IS YOUR WAY OF HIDING THE FACT THAT YOU'RE WORRIED, BUT PLEASE TRY NOT TO DISTRACT US FOR THE ENTIRE MISSION.

EVERYBODY FAN OUT AND STAY IN TOUCH.

STEEL TO SUPERGIRL. ELLESMERE ISLANDS CHECK OUT CLEAR. ANYTHING DRAMATIC HAPPENING IN THE SVALBARD REGION?

NOT UNLESS YOU COUNT A SEAL CUB SEPARATED FROM HIS MOTHER JUST OUTSIDE WEST SPITSBERGEN. WHAT ABOUT YOU, SUPERBOY?

WELL, I CAN'T MAKE ANY PROMISES--

--UNNNH!

SHUDDOOM!

--BUT I MIGHT HAVE FOUND SOMETHING TWO HUNDRED KILOMETERS WEST OF...umm...MOUNT FOREL.

WHAT'S UP, SON? SPOT A COUPLE OF SUSPICIOUS-LOOKING SNOWMEN?

WELL, AREN'T YOU THE FUNNY ONE!

THERE'S NOTHING ON A SUPERFICIAL LEVEL. I'M WORKING MY WAY UP THE ELECTROMAGNETIC SPECTRUM USING--

GOOD GOD!

GOT SOMETHING?

"YOU COULD SAY THAT."

WE'LL SPLIT UP ONCE WE'RE INSIDE. KEEP COM-LINKS OPEN.

FLUNK!

MY PSYCHIC LINK WITH THE MANHUNTER JUST BROKE DOWN, MEANING NOBODY EVEN KNOWS WE'RE IN HERE.

ANYONE THINK WE SHOULD BAIL OUT?

STEEL, WHOEVER GOT TO SUPERMAN HAS HIM TRAPPED IN HERE SOMEWHERE.

WHAT ELSE ARE WE SUPPOSED TO DO? DIAL 911? HE COULD BE DEAD BY THE TIME WE WAIT FOR THE JUSTICE LEAGUE TO--

BZZZT!

JOHN? WHAT HAPPENED TO SUPERGIRL?

SHE'S OFF-LINE. THERE'S NO RESPONSE. OF COURSE, THE ALLOYS IN HERE COULD BE INTERFERING WITH THE RADIO WAVES, BUT I'M START-ING TO GET THAT SKIN-CRAWLING FEELING...

ME, TOO.

TACTILE TELEKINESIS, DON'T FAIL ME NOW!

HHURCH

H.CHUNNG!

SORRY.

BATTERIES MUST HAVE GONE DEAD.

MAN, WHY DO YOU ALWAYS END UP TALKING LIKE AN EXTRA FROM AN ALIENS MOVIE WHEN YOU WEAR ONE OF THESE THINGS?

MORE IMPORTANT--

THE BATTERIES?

SUPERBOY TO STEEL: WE JUST HAD A LITTLE, ah, TECHNICAL PROBLEM DOWN HERE, BIG GUY. RESUME SEARCH. OVER AND OUT.

--WHY DO YOU ALWAYS TRY TO RESCUE ME WHEN I'M CLEARLY THE MOST POWERFUL OF THE THREE?

HEY, C'MON, DON'T GIVE ME THE BORING WONDER WOMAN SPEECH. WE'RE ALL SUPPOSED TO BE...

STEEL? WHATEVER IT WAS IMPERSONATING SUPERMAN...?

I THINK I JUST FOUND IT.

YOU'RE SMARTER THAN YOU PRETEND TO BE, SUPERBOY.

BUT NOT NEARLY SMART ENOUGH.

SHZAAKK!

STEEEEELL!

AAUGHH!

FOR GOD'S SAKE, LEAVE HIM ALONE!

HE'S JUST A BOY!

IS THAT SUPPOSED TO MAKE A DIFFERENCE, ah...?

WHAT IS IT THEY CALL YOU AGAIN? CANNED JUSTICE?

STEEL. HERE'S MY AUTOGRAPH.

NICE HAMMER.

FAPP

I SEE IT'S IMPREGNATED WITH THE SAME MATRIX OF MATERIALS AS THE ARMOR, BUT BECAUSE IT FORMS A THREE-DIMENSIONAL SOLID, THE EFFECTS ARE EVEN MORE INTERESTING.

LET'S SEE WHAT IT CAN REALLY DO.

SKKRRNNCH

YOU'RE WASTING YOUR TIME. I'VE GOT EVERY POWER YOU'VE EVER HEARD OF AND A THOUSAND THAT YOU HAVEN'T.

SUPER-SPEED, SUPER-HEARING, TELE-KINESIS, PYROKINESIS-- I'VE COLLECTED THEM ALL ON MY MAIN-FRAME, OVER COUNTLESS MILLENNIA...

SHAZZAAK!

SHORT-CIRCUIT VISION, TOO.

PUTTING UP A STRUGGLE REALLY JUST DELAYS THE INEVITABLE.

YOUR HEARTRATES ARE INCREASING, YOUR BREATHING IS GETTING FASTER, ELECTRICAL ACTIVITY IN YOUR BRAIN IS ALMOST UNRECOGNIZABLE FROM WHAT IT WAS ONLY MOMENTS AGO...

NOW THAT YOU'RE AWAKE, YOU MUST BE ASKING YOURSELVES WHO YOU'RE ACTUALLY DEALING WITH HERE.

YOU MUST BE WONDERING HOW THIS INDIVIDUAL YOU'VE NEVER SEEN BEFORE WAS ABLE TO CAPTURE AND DEFEAT FOUR OF THE MOST FORMIDABLE SUPER-HUMANS ON THE FACE OF THE EARTH.

SUPERMAN COULD ANSWER YOUR QUESTIONS. AT LEAST, HE COULD IF HE HADN'T BEEN SO TRAUMATIZED BY THE HORRORS I'VE PUT HIM THROUGH LATELY.

POOR LITTLE KRYPTONIAN...

...HE HASN'T SAID A WORD IN DAYS.

"THEY CALL ME THE ANTI-HERO. I KILL SUPER-HEROES...

"IT REALLY IS JUST AS SIMPLE AS THAT.

"THERE'S NO SECRET ORIGIN OF PARTICULAR INTEREST, NO DRAMATIC REVELATION WHERE I TURN OUT TO BE YOUR HALF BROTHER OR YOUR ARCH RIVAL OR ANY OF THOSE BORING OLD CLICHÉS.

"I JUST LIKE KILLING PEOPLE LIKE YOU."

GIANT ONES, SMALL ONES, SQUADRONS, LEAGUES OR SOCIETIES.

YOU ALL END UP HERE SOONER OR LATER, YOUR POWERS STORED ON MY COMPUTER TO BE ACCESSED WHENEVER I PLEASE.

I'M NOT EXACTLY SURE HOW MANY HEROES I'VE TORTURED AND KILLED OVER THE YEARS, BUT THERE'S ONE THING I'M ABSOLUTELY CERTAIN ABOUT...

...THE NUMBERS GO UP BY THREE TONIGHT.

"COMPUTER, PREPARE A LIST OF EVERY META-HUMAN CURRENTLY RESIDING ON PLANET EARTH AND HIGHLIGHT ANYONE INTERESTING WHO EXHIBITS ABILITIES I DON'T ALREADY HAVE."

SUPERGIRL? STEEL?

um, GUYS? WHAT DO YOU THINK?

I THINK THERE *MUST* BE SOME WAY OUT OF HERE.

YOU KNOW, EVEN IF JUST ONE OF US CAN GET OUT, WE CAN LET THE JLA KNOW WHERE WE ARE.

SUPERMAN'S OUR BEST BET. WE SHOULD AIM FOR HIM.

KID, DO YOU THINK YOU CAN TIP THESE CONTAINMENT UNITS?

...GOTTA PUSH MY TK AS FAR...

I MIGHT NOT BE ABLE TO BREAK WHATEVER'S HOLDING THESE THINGS--

TAP

--BUT THEY'RE *TIPPING!*

GREAT JOB, SUPERBOY! JOHN, WHAT'S NEXT?

IF I CAN SHORT THROUGH SOME OF THE MECHANISMS IN THE UNITS, ABSORB THE ENERGY FROM YOUR POD--

--YOU *MIGHT* BE ABLE TO GET OUT, SUPERGIRL.

¿uugghh¿

SIT TIGHT, GUYS. WE'RE NOT DONE YET.

I'VE GOTTA GET THROUGH THIS STUFF... IT'S TOUGHER THAN ANYTHING I'VE EVER HIT...

CLARK, PLEASE BE OKAY.

SUPERMAN... IT'S ALL ABOUT TEAMWORK... TAG, YOU'RE IT...

EEEARGHH!

WHAT?

NO.

TRAK

KOOM!

THIS IS IMPOSSIBLE!

HOW DID YOU BREAK OUT OF MY UNBREAKABLE CHAMBER?!

DO YOUR RESEARCH BETTER NEXT TIME, MISTER...

I'M SUPERMAN.

IT'S WHAT I DO.

DON'T MESS WITH THE *MAN*, CREEPAZOID!

I WOULDN'T GET TOO EXCITED. THIS ISN'T THE REGULAR TURNING POINT WHERE THE VILLAIN'S ON THE ROPES AND THE HEROES START TO GET THE UPPER HAND.

I... CAN'T SEE!

huh?

HE *BLINDED* ME!

I'M ONLY PLAYING WITH YOU.

SHOWING OFF MY POWERS.

GIVING YOU THE TINIEST GLIMPSE OF WHAT I'M CAPABLE OF DOING.

SUPER-SPEED, SUPER-STRENGTH, INVISIBILITY, INTANGIBILITY.

YOU'RE GOING TO BE BACK INSIDE YOUR LITTLE CELLS BEFORE YOU EVEN KNOW WHAT HIT YOU.

I DON'T NEED TO SEE YOU TO HEAR YOU COMING, MISTER.

BENEFITS OF SUPER-HEARING.

AARGHH!

SHRAAK!

SUPERGIRL, DON'T LET HIM GET BACK UP!

HIT HIM WITH A TELEKINETIC BLAST!

LET'S MAKE IT A DOUBLE!

ALWAYS WONDERED IF YOUR TK WOULD WORK WITH MINE.

CHOOOM!

I THINK THE SHOCK MUST HAVE LOOSENED HIS GRIP ON MY OPTIC NERVE. SOME COLORS ARE COMING BACK INTO FOCUS.

IS THIS A BAD TIME TO MAKE A JOKE ABOUT THE BLONDE LEADING THE BLIND?

AAAA!

WHAT HAVE YOU DONE TO MY INVULNERABILITY?

THAT HURT!

CHUKT!

THAT ACTUALLY HURT!

GOOD GOD! STEEL--!

STEEL'S DOWN!

SK ISH

TAKE IT EASY, PEOPLE. OCCUPY HIS ATTENTION FOR ANOTHER TEN SECONDS AND I'LL HAVE THIS PIECE OF GARBAGE DISCONNECTED FROM EVERY SUPER-POWER IN HIS MAIN FRAME.

THE POSITIVE SIDE OF THE SUIT'S BEING DECAPITATED IS THAT I CAN WORK EIGHTY PERCENT FASTER WHEN I'M NOT OPERATING THE ARMOR USING THE REMOTE FUNCTION.

WE'RE STILL ON SCHEDULE.

DON'T LISTEN TO HIM!

DO YOU REALIZE HOW MANY POWERS I'VE STILL GOT ACCESS TO UP THERE?

HAVE YOU ANY IDEA HOW MANY DIFFERENT WAYS I CAN KILL YOU USING POWERS YOU DON'T EVEN HAVE WORDS FOR?

I'M GOING TO SQUEEZE ALL FOUR OF YOU INTO THAT ARMOR OF HIS AND THEN I'M GOING AFTER THE REST OF THEM.

I'M GOING TO SNAP EVERY GRAVITY ROD, MELT EVERY MAGIC HELMET, MAKE GREEN LANTERN EAT HIS OWN RING!

I'M GOING TO LACE EVERY OXYGEN MOLECULE ON THIS PLANET WITH A COCKTAIL OF BUBONIC PLAUGE AND BILHARZIA PARASITES!

51

HE'S ON HIS OWN, BOYS AND GIRLS.

SHUT HIM DOWN WHENEVER YOU FEEL LIKE IT.

OH, THIS ISN'T OVER YET, SUPERMAN. NOT BY A LONG SHOT.

URRF!

I WAS KILLING CAPES WHEN THE PEOPLE OF KRYPTON WERE STILL RUNNING AROUND ON ALL FOURS.

HALF A MILLION BATTLES AND I'VE STILL NEVER BEEN BEATEN!

WHAT DO YOU HAVE TO SAY TO THAT, "SUPER-HERO"?

RRRIIIIIPP!

THERE'S A FIRST TIME FOR EVERY-THING.

NO!

D-DON'T HURT ME, SUPERMAN! WITHOUT MY EXOSKELETON, I'M JUST A DEFENSELESS INVERTEBRATE! YOU'RE RE-NOWNED ACROSS THIS WORLD AS A MAN WHO ANSWERS CRIES FOR HELP...

EW!

...THEN TAKE PITY ON ME NOW, KRYPTONIAN.

HELP ME!

S.T.A.R. LABS...

PUTTING THE ANTI-HERO IN A V.R. CHAMBER WHERE HE CAN BE CHEMICALLY-REHABILITATED SEEMS LIKE SUCH A TOTALLY "SUPERMAN" THING TO DO, *huh?*

I MEAN. IF I'D SUFFERED HALF OF WHAT SUPES WENT THROUGH, I RECKON MY FIRST REACTION WOULD HAVE BEEN TO SQUISH THE LITTLE SLEAZE.

THAT'S WHY WE WEAR THE SYMBOL ON OUR CHESTS, SUPER-BOY--TO REMIND US WHAT WE CAN *ASPIRE* TO SOMEDAY.

OR WHAT WE'RE CAPABLE OF *NOW*, JOHN.

YOU KNOW, I WEAR THE SYMBOL 'CAUSE IT MATCHES MY PANTS.

SPEAKING OF BIG BLUE...

...IT'S A SHAME HE DIDN'T HAVE TIME TO GRAB A COFFEE AFTER WE DESTROYED THE SHIP, BUT I GUESS HE'S NOT EXACTLY FAMOUS FOR RELAXING.

HE'S PROBABLY GIVING WGBS THE FULL STORY OR SOMETHING.

BUT HAVEN'T YOU NOTICED HOW SUPERMAN ALWAYS DISAPPEARS AFTER AN EMERGENCY? WHERE DO YOU THINK HE GOES?

OH, YOU KNOW HOW IT IS IN THIS BUSINESS, JOHN...

DOESN'T ANYONE ELSE THINK IT'S KIND OF SUSPICIOUS?

"...WE ALL NEED OUR SECRETS."

END

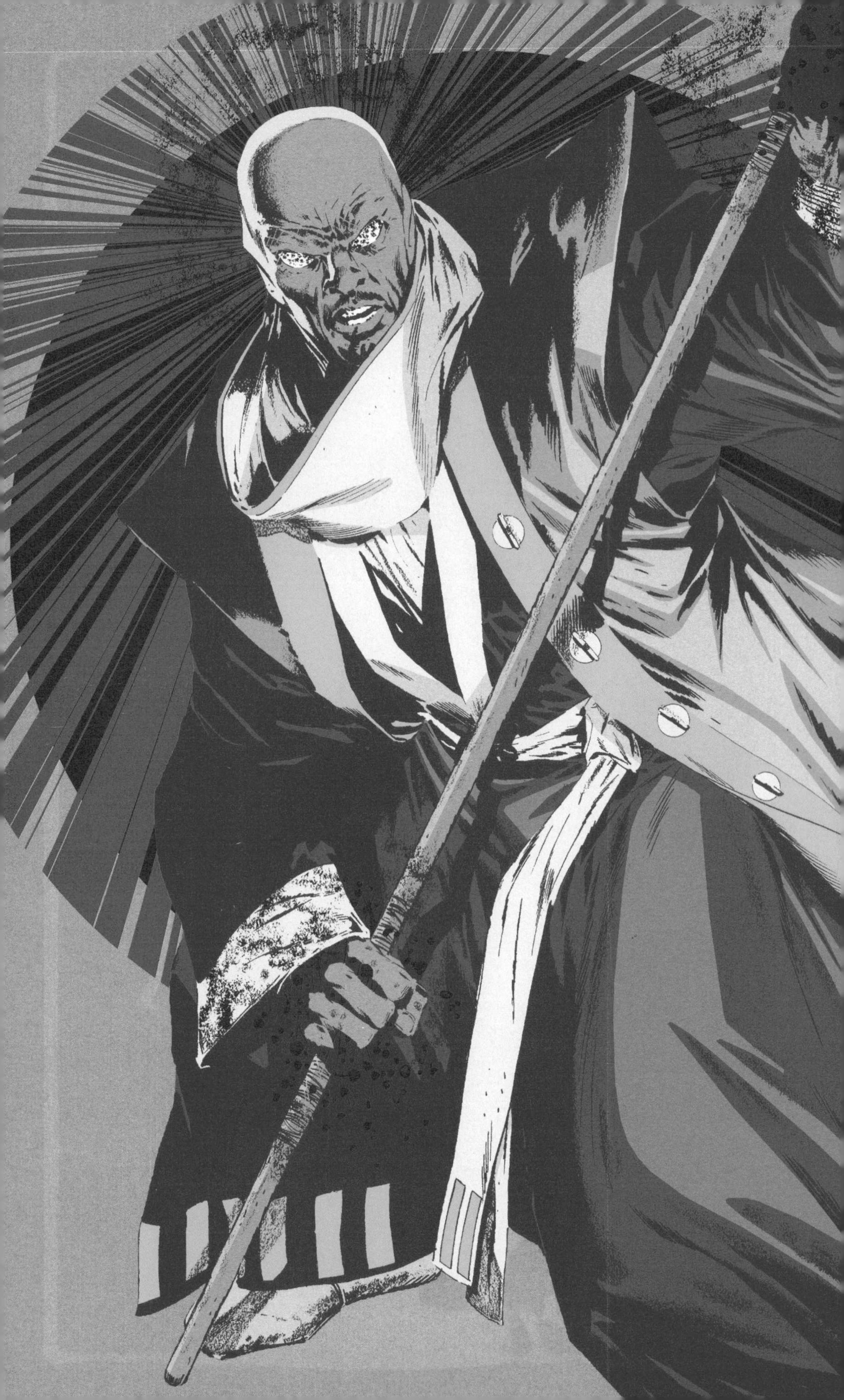

The details of how we ended up like this are so vast and complex, I barely know where to start, but I suppose the day he was born is as good a place as any.

His mother was induced shortly before the Nixon assassination by military doctors in a Nightwing base which never existed outside blurred pictures in the tabloids.

His father was screaming in the next room with mouths surfacing on his body faster than any-one could count.

This sweet little Nativity was attended by a dozen of the most highly-decorated military servicemen in the country, armed to the teeth and ready to open fire on whatever came out if it chose to attack.

The mother died giving birth to a perfectly normal nine-pound baby boy the authorities named Harvey Lee Dent.

But they needn't have bothered.

Nothing of any significance happened for the next twenty-three years.

FUTURE SHOCK

MARK MILLAR
Story

JACKSON GUICE
Art

LOVERN KINDZIERSKI
Colorist

DIGITAL CHAMELEON
Separations

COMICRAFT
Letters

FRANK BERRIOS
Assistant Editor

EDDIE BERGANZA
Editor

Special thanks to
JOE ILLIDGE

TANGENT
BASED ON
CONCEPTS BY
DAN JURGENS

I'M WARNING YOU, OFFICER: TAKE *ONE* MORE STEP FORWARD AND I TAKE ONE SIDEWAYS.

THIS IS NOT A NEGOTIABLE SITUATION.

IT'S OKAY, RELAX. I GET THE PICTURE.

THAT *FRANK SINATRA/ DIRTY HARRY* STUFF AIN'T MY STYLE, CARTER.

I'M A *DESK JOCKEY* WITH A STOMACH ULCER AND A FEAR OF HEIGHTS SO BAD MY GIRLFRIEND CHANGES THE LIGHT BULBS, MAN.

I'M ONLY HERE TO *TALK,*

POLICE OFFICER HARVEY DENT TO *ARCHITECT* CARTER HALL.

HOW COULD HE PICK *YELLOW?* MY DRAWINGS SPECIFIED A TASTEFUL *TERRACOTTA,* BUT BRANDE HAS TURNED THE TALLEST BUILDING IN THE WORLD INTO A BANANA WITH *FINS,*

I'M A *LAUGHING* STOCK!

I'M NOT LAUGHING, CARTER. IN FACT, MY LEGS ARE SHAKING SO BAD I'M PRACTICALLY IN *TEARS* HERE, MAN. HOLD MY HAND...

KLKKT

WHAT THE *HELL* IS THIS?

A TEXT-BOOK EXAMPLE OF SMART THINKING, HAIR-BALL.

THERE'S NO WAY YOU'RE GOING SKY-DIVING NOW UNLESS YOU PLAN ON TAKING *ME* WITH YOU AND, FRANKLY, YOU DON'T SMELL LIKE THE *HOMICIDAL* VARIETY TO ME.

SON OF A --

SLIGHT MISCALCULATION.

CARTER, NO!

MARY, MOTHER OF GOD.

THRUNCH

HARD DAY ON PATROL, DEAR?

NO SWEAT FOR THE NEIGHBOR-HOODS NUMBER-ONE HERO, HONEY. SAY, I HOPE YOU DIDN'T FORGET --

-- THE SEVEN SOLDIERS OF VICTORY ARE COMING OVER FOR DINNER TONIGHT.

I'VE TOLD ALL THE BOYS WHAT A SWELL COOK YOU ARE.

GULP! I HOPE YOU HAD YOUR FINGERS CROSSED.

Oh, MY GOSH! YOU'VE BURNED THE CASSEROLE WITH YOUR LASER-VISION AND THE SEVEN SOLDIERS OF VICTORY WILL BE HERE ANY MINUTE! WOULD IT BE UNPATRIOTIC OF ME TO ORDER CHINESE?

DINNER'S THE LEAST OF YER WORRIES, MASTER. SOME CRIMINAL GENIUS JUST BROKE OUTTA JAIL AN' COATED MY DOG BISCUITS IN A SUPER-LAXATIVE. YA DON'T WANNA HEAR WHAT HAPPENED WHEN I FLEW OVER TOWN TODAY!

WHAT? ARE YOU GUYS TRYING TO RUIN MY CHANCE OF JOINING THIS TEAM?

ALL I NEED NOW IS RICHIE TO TELL ME THE SUPER-VILLAINS NEXT DOOR USED THEIR WEIRD POWERS TO TURN HIM INTO AN INSECTOID OR SOMETHING!

DAD, YOU'RE NOT GONNA LIKE THIS.

WHAT KIND OF IMPRESSION IS THIS GOING TO MAKE ON THE GUYS!

I'LL BE DOING LAME TEAM-UPS WITH THE MIND-GRABBER KID FOR THE REST OF MY LIFE!

HEY, IF THE IDEA OF SHOTS DON'T SCARE YA, THE LEGION OF SUPER-PETS IS ALWAYS LOOKIN' FOR NEW MEMBERS, BIG GUY!

61

MAN, THE *DICK VAN HERO SHOW* SURE WENT DOWNHILL WHEN THEY INTRODUCED THAT LAME DOG IN THE MASK. HARD TO BELIEVE THIS CRAP MADE ME WANT TO BE A COP WHEN I WAS A KID.

LOOKS LIKE YOU'VE GOT VISITORS, MR. DENT.

HEY, BABY. ABOUT TIME I SAW A PRETTY FACE AROUND HERE.

WHAT DID I TELL YOU, LOLA? ONLY THIS CLOWN COULD JUMP OFF THE TALLEST BUILDING IN THE WORLD AND HIT THE GROUND WITHOUT A SCRATCH.

OHMYGOD, HARVEY...

C'MON, PIE-FACE. I LOOK LIKE I BEEN IN THE RING WITH *THE ATOM.*

MRS. DENT, THE MAN HE WAS HAND-CUFFED TO TURNED INSIDE OUT WHEN HE HIT THE SIDEWALK. WE COULDN'T EVEN IDENTIFY HIM FROM HIS DENTAL RECORDS.

AS FAR AS THE FORENSIC PEOPLE ARE CONCERNED, YOUR HUSBAND SHOULD HAVE BEEN *HOSED OFF* THE ROOF OF THAT POLICE CAR.

Oh, WE AIN'T MARRIED, DOCTOR REGULUS. SHE'S STILL PLAIN OLD MISS BARNETT UNTIL SHE SUCKERS SOMEONE INTO PUTTING A RING ON HER FINGER.

AS IF I'D TAKE A WALK DOWN THE AISLE WITH A MIDDLE-INCOME BLUE-COLLAR WORKER WITH PROSPECTS AS BLEAK AS YOURS, HARVEY DENT.

I TOLD YOU I'M GOING TO MARRY A MAN WITH LETTERS AFTER HIS NAME.

WELL, ACCORDING TO THESE CHARTS, *SUPERMAN* HERE SHOULD HAVE HAD THE LETTERS *R.I.P.* AFTER HIS NAME, BUT IT LOOKS LIKE THE GOOD LORD HAD BIGGER PLANS FOR HARVEY DENT.

Harvey had always been the kind of guy who didn't know how to wire an electric plug, but the weeks that followed saw him take apart and re-build practically everything we had in our apartment.

Of course, at this stage, I just assumed he was either bored sitting around all day with nothing to do or his brush with death had given him a new appreciation for learning.

The fact that he even knew where the library was surprised me, but when he said he'd re-read every book on their shelves in a week, I nearly asked to check his ID to make sure I was sleeping with the right guy.

I mean, this was the man who found Dr. Seuss challenging, and here he was reading Descartes faster than he could turn the page.

By the time he went back to work, Harvey had devised a whole new method of policing, but the other cops were a little resistant to his radical proposals.

Until they discovered crime on his beat was virtually nonexistent.

It was around this time he stopped sleeping and I was starting to get a little worried about him.

LOLA!

HARVEY, WHAT'S WRONG?

LOLA! COME QUICKLY!

Oh, MY GOD! I'M COMING! I'M COMING!

HARVEY!

I'M OUT THE WINDOW, BABY!

LOOK! LOOK!

At this stage, we still weren't sure whether the extra-normal abilities Harvey was developing had been caused by the accident or whether the fall just triggered something that had always been there.

Whatever, pyrokinesis was kind of romantic...

Telekinesis was a scream...

Telepathy and premonitions of the future (I'm not sure what to call that. ESP?) caused Harvey the most anxiety when he realized for the first time how much his co-workers were beginning to resent him.

This is when he decided he should pretend to be a normal person again, particularly during working hours.

But at night he could be himself and enjoy the fact that his brain was evolving at the rate of a century an hour, pondering why this was happening to him and to him alone.

Harvey realized he had an aptitude for solving other people's problems, and his cop's salary meant we lived in a neighborhood where there were plenty of problems to solve.

Crime, poor housing conditions, businesses finding it hard to stay afloat under President Schwartz's high interest rate policy.

Harvey became a regular Santa Claus, secretly helping anyone who e-mailed him with a problem he considered worthy.

He quickly became another urban myth, romanticized by the poor and the destitute.

They called him the Superman, but the truth was that most New Yorkers refused to believe in him and, as you might expect, he was clever enough to keep it that way for a while.

But Harvey was getting smarter every day and, before long, dealing with lost pets and abusive landlords didn't stimulate him as much as it used to and he began responding mostly to meta-human crises.

The Home-Boy Legion, Two-Face the master of disguise, the Spectral Hourman the cops couldn't touch 23 hours a day.

New York's weather-manipulating Heat-Wave, the grotesque Batgirl, Star Boy, the solar delinquent, Native American super-villain Johnny Thunder and his subservient Lightning-Bolt.

He figured out their weaknesses and beat them all one by one. I'd never seen him look so alive.

Harvey's first encounter with another superhero occurred when he answered an e-mail from the Coast Guard and ended up bumping into that new Atom, the hero they're always reporting about in World's Finest.

They teamed up to fight a crazy scientist called Dr. Martin Stein, who fused his brain with a nuclear submarine and re-christened himself Dr. Polaris, I think.

The Atom later gave details of their conversation in a Karl Ferris interview and publicly declared his doubts about whether the intentions of this mysterious Superman were as altruistic as they should be.

Harvey was becoming visibly colder and more remote every day, and it was obvious to anyone who spoke to him that he wasn't helping people because he liked to play the good Samaritan.

He just liked solving problems.

Every problem except one.

IF YOU'RE GOING TO TELEKINETICALLY *MUTILATE* YOURSELF, I'D RATHER IT WASN'T OVER THE KITCHEN TABLE IN THE FUTURE.

I'M NOT MUTILATING MYSELF, LOLA, I'M JUST *ALTERING* MY PHYSIOLOGY FOR TWENTY-FOUR HOURS TO GIVE ME THE POWERS I NEED TO DEFEAT THE SWAMP THING.

WHAT'S THE *MATTER* WITH YOU, HARVEY?

WHY CAN'T YOU USE THAT STUPID SUPER-INTELLIGENCE OF YOURS TO HELP *US* FOR A CHANGE AND MAYBE GET US OUT OF THIS CRAPPY APARTMENT?

THIS APARTMENT IS AS BIG AS IT'S ALWAYS BEEN, HONEY, AND IT'S NOT LIKE WE HAVE ANY FINANCIAL PROBLEMS. WHAT EXACTLY DO YOU WANT FROM ME?

A LITTLE COMPANIONSHIP, SOME ADULT CONVERSATION, A *SEX-LIFE.*

I *SLEPT* WITH PIE-FACE, HARVEY.

IT WAS A MISTAKE. WE AGREE IT'S NEVER GOING TO HAPPEN AGAIN, BUT, GOD FORGIVE ME, I JUST NEEDED A *LITTLE* COMPANY.

LOLA, I'M A *TELEPATH.*

I *KNEW* YOU WERE GOING TO SLEEP WITH PIE-FACE BEFORE YOU DID.

68

Harvey never entirely bought the theory that his accelerated evolution had been caused by the accident and had been looking into his origins for some time when the ex-Nightwing operative contacted him.

YAH *LATE*, SUPERMAN. DIDN'T YAH MAMA EVAH TELL YOU IT'S BAD MANNERS T'KEEP A LADY WAITIN'?

THE ARRANGEMENT IS THAT PEOPLE E-MAIL ME THEIR REQUESTS, MISS St. GEORGE, NOT ATTEMPT TO BREAK AND ENTER INTO MY SUBCONSCIOUS. STAY *OUT* OF MY HEAD IN THE FUTURE OR FACE THE CONSEQUENCES.

HONEY, IF YAH WASN'T SUCH A HANDSOME MAN, AH DO DECLARE AH'D HAVE TAKEN A DISLIKE TO YA BY NOW AND SEEIN' HOW THIS IS OFFICIAL BUSINESS, AH'D APPRECIATE YOU OBSERVIN' MAH BLACK ORCHID CODE NAME.

UNLESS Y'ALL WOULD PREFER YAH AN' ME TRADED INFORMATION ON A SOMEWHAT LESS OFFICIAL CAPACITY.

YOU SAID YOU HAD INFORMATION REGARDING MY ORIGINS, ORCHID...

...BUT THE ONLY DATA I'M PICKING UP FROM A CURSORY BRAIN-SCAN IS A MAP GIVEN TO YOU BY ONE OF YOUR TERRORIST SUPERIORS.

WE DON'T HAVE LEADERS IN OUR TEAM, SUGAH.

ONE OF THE BIG DIFFERENCES BETWEEN THE ROGUES AN' TH' BAD GUYS.

THIS LI'L MAP DETAILS THE PRECISE LOCATION OF TH'SECRET NIGHTWING BASE WHERE ALL THE QUESTIONS Y'ALL EVER WANTED TO ASK ABOUT YOURSELF CAN BE ANSWERED, SUPERMAN. JUST BE SURE T'LET 'EM KNOW WHO SENT YAH.

WHEN YAH TEAR THEM A NEW HOLE, AH MEAN.

WHAT?

WHEN YAH KILL THEM, SILLY BOY!

I DON'T THINK YOU UNDERSTAND. THIS ISN'T A DEAL. I'M NOT ACCEPTING THIS INFORMATION ON THE CONDITION THAT I HAVE TO MURDER ANYONE.

THE HERO

MAYBE NOT RIGHT NOW. AH CAN ACCEPT THAT, BUT IF EVEN HALF THE RUMORS AH HEARD BEFORE AH TOOK A WALK ARE TRUE...

...WELL, LET'S JUST SAY AH'M CONFIDENT YA'LL SHOULD DO THE RIGHT THING.

Until recently, Nightwing was so many levels above Top Secret, not even the President was aware of their existence.

Before being shut down, some Internet groups speculated on the location of Nightwing's many secret bases, with reports ranging from the Arctic Circle to mysterious caves beneath the Atomic Burger restaurants.

The command center in question was somewhere off the map entirely, outside all known forms of radar.

WHHOOOOM

Harvey must have been the last thing they were expecting.

Telepathically decoding their hard drives was no more difficult than receiving and reading the e-mails from around the world he stored at a virtual web address in his left frontal lobe.

Nightwing's biggest secrets tumbled one by one.

Details of a sincere, well-intentioned man began to emerge, a Professor Joseph Chill who had earlier been part of the team that produced the original Atom --

-- and now wanted to take the project one stage further in the face of mounting Soviet aggression.

Chill selected a small Southern town in the middle of nowhere, populated mostly by African Americans, as the petri dish for an experiment he hoped would transform America into the first superhuman nation.

His idea was to infect the water supply with a formula he developed called the Miraclo Solution which would accelerate the natural evolutionary process within the population.

The year was 1973.

Welcome to VICEROY S.C. POP. 803

Eighteen months later, half the population was screaming in agony as their brains turned to jelly.

The others half-mutated into some kind of hybrids representing almost everything on the evolutionary scale.

Chill was devastated.

Harvey himself entered the world as his mother departed, a perfectly healthy nine-pound baby who exhibited none of the deformities, but none of the special abilities Chill desired either.

The operation was considered a failure and an inquiry was launched.

Chill took the blame, keeping his Nightwing affiliation secret despite an intense grilling by a congressional committee and a promise from Richard Nixon that he would personally see him behind bars for life.

Naturally, Chill walked free and the Nixon administration was brought down by Nightwing just a few weeks later.

The strange thing is Chill would have been hailed as a hero if his operation had been a success. The Miraclo Solution would have given America a biological advantage over the entire world.

He wanted to create a race of Supermen...

...but ended up murdering an entire community and being written into the history books as one of the century's greatest monsters.

I guess America just doesn't like losers.

What came next for the town was almost humane.

Chill disappeared in 1976, twenty years before the nine-pound baby took a fall and triggered the evolutionary process within himself the professor had always fantasized about.

They say a photograph of Joseph Chill as an old man exists dated 1933, which probably isn't true, but he certainly wasn't anywhere to be found on the day Harvey came along looking for answers.

I can't imagine how frightening it must have been for those Nightwing people watching him silently pore over the details of what they had done. Who knows what was going on in their heads?

Besides Harvey, of course.

I didn't even ask what happened next.

It's been three days since I've seen him. I suppose all I am to Harvey now is the final souvenir from his former life.

I'd like to say I hate him for that, but the truth is I'm still madly in love with the guy.

That's why I'm putting this e-mail together.

He's always telling me every problem has a solution, how we can achieve anything if we put our minds to it. Well, let's see if he can solve this one. Can he devise a plan to save our relationship?

There's no harm in asking, and they say the Man of Tomorrow can never ignore a genuine cry for help.

Help.

NEW ADDRESS ATTACH SEND DELETE

He's always telling me every problem has a solution, how we can achieve anything if we put our minds to it. Well, let's see if he can solve this one. Can he devise a plan to save our relationship? There's no harm in asking, and they say the Man of Tomorrow can never ignore a genuine cry for help.

WORLD GREATE LOVE

I SEE YOU'VE BEEN PACKING.

PIE-FACE ASKED ME IF I WANTED TO MOVE TO NEW ATLANTIS WITH HIM. HE SAID YOU WERE A LOSER AND I DESERVED BETTER THAN SITTING HOME EVERY NIGHT WATCHING TV ON MY OWN.

GOOD OLD PIE-FACE, HUH?

I *DON'T* LOVE HIM, HARVEY. THE TRUTH IS I DON'T EVEN *LIKE* HIM, BUT HE LOOKS AT ME THE WAY *YOU* USED TO AND I *NEED* THAT KIND OF ATTENTION FOR A WHILE.

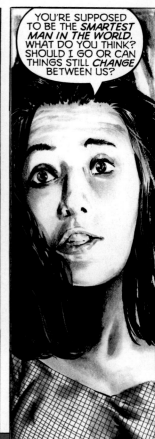

YOU'RE SUPPOSED TO BE THE *SMARTEST MAN IN THE WORLD.* WHAT DO YOU THINK? SHOULD I GO OR CAN THINGS STILL *CHANGE* BETWEEN US?

THINGS CAN ALWAYS CHANGE. WE'RE ONLY LIMITED BY OUR IMAGINATIONS.

WHAT'S THIS? AND WHY ARE YOU WEARING *THAT?*

I CAN NEVER GO BACK, LOLA. IT WOULD BE LIKE ASKING YOU TO DRAG YOUR KNUCKLES ACROSS THE FLOOR WHEN YOU WALK.

IT WOULD HURT TOO MUCH AFTER EVERYTHING I'VE SEEN, BUT I CAN *TAKE* YOU WHEREVER I'M GOING.

JUST *SWALLOW* THE MIRACLO PILL AND *JOIN* ME.

SWALLOW A CHEMICAL THAT *KILLED* A WHOLE TOWN?

GREAT IDEA, HARVEY! NO WONDER THEY CALL YOU THE SMARTEST MAN ALIVE.

QUIET.

HEY, WHAT HAPPENED TO THE LIGHTS?

AN ELECTROMAGNETIC PULSE OF ULTRA-TERRESTRIAL ORIGIN DISRUPTING ELECTRIC FIELDS FROM ONE END OF THE GLOBE TO THE OTHER.

COME AGAIN?

"AN ENERGY WAVE SPREADING OUT ACROSS THE GLOBE AND SHUTTING DOWN EVERYTHING THAT IDENTIFIED US AS A TWENTIETH-CENTURY SOCIETY: EVERY ENGINE, EVERY LIGHT-BULB, EVERY MEANS OF COMMUNICATION...

"...SOMETHING TERRIBLE JUST ENTERED THE WORLD AND MADE EVERYTHING SICK. I CAN FEEL IT TAKING ITS FIRST BREATH RIGHT NOW SOMEWHERE IN THE SOVIET UNION. IT ALREADY HAS A NAME, LOLA...

"...IT CALLS ITSELF THE ULTRA-HUMANITE."

THE LIGHTS ARE BACK ON.

ONLY BECAUSE IT'S DIFFICULT TO HOLD A MEANINGFUL CONVERSATION IN THE DARK. I BELIEVE WE WERE TALKING ABOUT YOU JOINING ME IN SUPER-HUMANITY.

HARVEY, *STOP* MESSING AROUND WITH MY HEAD. YOU WERE TALKING ABOUT THIS ULTRA-HUMANITE MONSTER. DON'T YOU HAVE TO STOP IT OR SOMETHING?

I'M NOT *INTERESTED* IN THE ULTRA-HUMANITE. I'M INTERESTED IN *YOU.*

THERE'S NO RISK, LOLA. I *ELIMINATED* THE FLAWS IN PROFESSOR CHILL'S ORIGINAL FORMULA. SWALLOW THE CAPSULE NOW AND YOU'LL HAVE EVOLVED A MILLION YEARS BY *TONIGHT.* WE CAN DO THIS TOGETHER. MR. AND MRS. SUPERMAN.

IT WOULD BE LIKE THE DICK VAN HERO SHOW.

WHY ARE YOU DOING THIS, HARVEY? HONESTLY.

BECAUSE I LOVE YOU, BABY. IT CAN GET SO LONELY IN HERE. I WANT TO SAVE THIS RELATIONSHIP AS MUCH AS YOU DO. I SWEAR ON MY LIFE.

GOOD.

BECAUSE I'D HATE TO THINK THIS WAS JUST ANOTHER PROBLEM YOU WANTED TO PROVE YOU WERE CAPABLE OF SOLVING.

END

SYSTEM'S FINEST
BATMAN SUPERMAN

YOU SAW THE EVIDENCE ON THE *SUPER-ORACLE,* HEARTIAC. UNLESS I DISGUISE MYSELF AS *ALCHEMO,* THE ENTIRE *SYSTEM* IS DOOMED.

I DON'T *GET* IT, BATMAN. WHY DO YOU NEED TO DRESS UP LIKE *PICO-MOTH?* THIS DIRTBAG'S ONE OF YOUR *WORST* ENEMIES.

CONGRATULATIONS! YOU HAVE SOURCED ONE OF THE MOST REVERED INFO-CAPSULES IN HEADNET'S ARCHIVES.

PREPARE TO BE THRILLED BY THE ORIGIN OF THE *SYSTEM'S FINEST* DUO IN A CLASSIC *COSMIC ENCOUNTER* FILED UNDER THE HEADING...

"*WE HAVE SEEN THE ENEMY—AND THEY ARE US!*"

MARK MILLAR-STORY MIKE WIERINGO-PENCILS RICHARD CASE-INKS
TIM HARKINS - LETTERS   FELIX SERRANO- COLORS

79

THE ASYLUM PLANET OF PLUTO, 85,267 A.D.:

WE'RE *GAINING* ON HIM, BOSS! LET'S SHOW THIS CREEP NOBODY BUSTS OUTTA THE CLINK WHEN *BATMAN AND ROBIN* ARE ON DUTY!

MAKE SURE YOU'RE STRAPPED INTO THE *OMNI-BAT*, TOY WONDER. I'M ABOUT TO MULTIPLY *SPEED* BY A FACTOR OF *TEN.*

RELEASE THE SNARE!

GOTCHA!

VRRRRT!

DEET!

BATMAN! TOY WONDER! I KNOW HOW THIS LOOKS, BUT YOU'VE GOT TO BELIEVE I WASN'T PLANNING TO MAKE AN *OFF-WORLD JUMP.*

IT WAS, *uh*, JUST GETTING A LITTLE CLAUSTROPHOBIC IN THAT NANO-CHIP YOU GUYS TRAPPED ME INSIDE.

HEY! WHAT DO WE LOOK LIKE... *BIZARROS?*

FIVE PIVOTAL MEMBERS OF THE BATMAN REVENGE SQUAD HAVE TRIED TO ESCAPE DURING THE LAST SIXTY MINUTES.

YOU'RE GOING TO TELL ME *WHY*, PICO-MOTH.

THE FORTRESS OF SOLITUDE, TESSERACT SPACE.

DEFEATING ALCHEMO USING SHEER *KINDNESS* WAS A SIGHT TO BEHOLD, HEARTIAC.

I'VE NEVER SEEN A SENTIENT CRY LIKE THAT BEFORE...

I HOPE YOU DON'T MIND MY ANSWERING THE SUPER-ORACLE ALARM BEFORE WE BOOM-SUIT THIS FELLOW BACK TO PLUTO.

NOT AT ALL, SUPERMAN. WE BOTH KNOW YOUR DESCENDANTS ONLY CONTACT YOU IN CASES OF THE MOST EXTREME *URGENCY.*

WHAT'S THE PROBLEM, SON ?

HUNTER'S LAW OF TIME FORBIDS ME FROM DIVULGING THE SPECIFICS, SUPERMAN, BUT YOU MUST DO EXACTLY AS I SAY OR ALL IS LOST.

OUR FUTURE DEMANDS YOU ASSUME ALCHEMO'S IDENTITY AND ATTEND A MEETING OF THE SUPERMAN REVENGE SQUAD IN DEEP SPACE.

A TRIP INTO SPACE MEANS I'LL MISS YOUR FORGIVENESS LECTURE TO THE SUPER-TEENS AT METROPOLIS MULTIVERSITY, HEARTIAC.

MAYBE I'D BE MORE ANNOYED IF MY ANCESTORS HADN'T HAD AN IDEOLOGICAL SPLIT WITH OUR CEREBRAL COUSINS, SUPERMAN.

FORTUNATELY, YOU'RE TALKING TO A TWELFTH-LEVEL COMPASSIONATE, AND DISAPPOINTMENT ISN'T EVEN PART OF MY LEXICON.

SOB! IF ONLY THAT BIG DOPE KNEW HOW I *REALLY* FELT ABOUT HIM.

81

HARDWARE UPDATE! THE VESSEL YOU'RE SOURCING IS A TRANS-DIMENSIONAL LINER USED TO MOVE STUDENTS AND CARGO BETWEEN THE THIRD AND FIFTH DIMENSIONS

THE VARANIA IS AN UNMANNED CRAFT BUT CAN BE SEEN HERE AS A MEETING PLACE FOR ONE HUNDRED DEADLY SUPER-VILLAINS.

POINT OF IRONY: A DISGUISED SUPERMAN AND BATMAN TALK TO ONE ANOTHER WITHOUT REALIZING THEIR HIDDEN IDENTITIES.

I'M SURPRISED TO FIND YOU HERE, ALCHEMO. I'D HEARD THIS WAS A MEETING FOR THE BATMAN REVENGE SQUAD.

ACTUALLY, PICO-MOTH, THEY TOLD ME IT WAS A CONVENTION FOR PEOPLE WHO WANTED TO THROTTLE SUPERMAN.

THE TRUTH IS THAT YOU'RE *BOTH* RIGHT, GENTLEMEN...

GREAT SCOTT!

FOR ANYONE WHO DOESN'T KNOW, MY NAME IS *OWAC* AND MY PARTNER IN CRIME HERE CALLS HIMSELF THE LAUGHING VIRUS.

WE'VE COME TO OFFER YOU A CHANCE TO BECOME FIVE-DIMENSIONAL IMPS AND DESTROY SUPERMAN AND BATMAN FOREVER, KIDDIES.

NO JOKE!

82

HEADNET INTERLUDE! SUPERMAN/BATMAN ARCHRIVALS.

OWAC: ONE WOMAN ADVERSARY CHAMBER. THE GENIUS OF THE SUPERMAN DYNASTY'S GREATEST FOES CAN BE ACCESSED VIA THE ICONS SITUATED ALONG THE RIGHT ARM OF HER PRISON FATIGUES.

REAL NAME: LORI LOMBARD-THUROL. HER HATRED OF SUPERMAN STEMS FROM BELIEVING SHE WAS DESTINED TO BE HIS TRUE LOVE UNTIL HEARTIAC WAS TRANSFERRED TO METROPOLIS MULTIVERSITY.

DEFINING MOMENT: WITNESSING HIM WINK AT HER IN A HISTORICAL LEARNING TESSERACT AND VOWING SUPERMAN'S ABSOLUTE DESTRUCTION.

QUOTE: "MY ONLY LOVE NOW IS PURE REASON."

THE LAUGHING VIRUS: BELIEVED TO BE THE GHOST OF THE ORIGINAL BATMAN'S GREATEST FOE, MURDERED IN THE 21st CENTURY.

MOTIVATION: EMBITTERED BECAUSE THE DARK KNIGHT FAILED TO SAVE HIS LIFE, THE COSMIC CLOWN OF HATE SWORE HE'D TORMENT THE BATMAN LEGACY UNTIL HE FELT HIS INJUSTICE HAD BEEN AVENGED.

ABILITIES: PSYCHIC POSSESSION OF MAN OR MACHINE.

QUOTE: "HAHAHAHAHA!"

83

THE VIRUS'S UNIQUE ABILITY TO INFILTRATE *ANY* COMPUTER COMBINED WITH *MY GENIUS* MEANT WE WERE ABLE TO HIJACK THE VARANIA AND MEET THE FIFTH-DIMENSIONAL *GENIES* WE'VE BEEN SPEAKING TO.

GENIES WHO PROMISED TO UPGRADE EACH AND EVERY ONE OF US TO IMP STATUS IF WE SUPPLY *THEM* WITH A CERTAIN COMMODITY.

BUT WHAT COULD WE POSSIBLY OFFER FIVE-DIMENSIONAL CRIMINALS, *OWAC*? THOSE GUYS CAN HAVE ANYTHING THEY WANT.

OH, BUT THAT'S WHERE YOU'RE WRONG, PICO-MOTH.

THERE'S SOMETHING WE HAVE IN *ABUNDANCE* WHICH YOU'LL FIND IS *FORBIDDEN CURRENCY* IN THE FIFTH DIMENSION, MY FRIEND.

LADIES AND GENTLEMEN, WE'RE TALKING ABOUT OUR *VOWELS.*

THAT'S ALL I NEEDED TO *HEAR!*

uh-oh! *TROUBLE* ONBOARD!

TROUBLE TIMES *TWO,* MISTER! NICE TO MEET YOU, SUPERMAN.

GOSH! SUPERMAN *AND* BATMAN! SOUNDS LIKE THE WORST DINNER PARTY IMAGINABLE. GOOD THING *I'M* PILOTING THE 5-D EXPRESS, CLOAKED CRUSADERS...

"... OTHERWISE, WE MIGHT HAVE *MISSED* THIS KRYPTONITE CITY AS WE TRAVEL THROUGH THE *TIME-WARP* SOME EGGHEADS CALL THE *FOURTH DIMENSION.*"

YOU MANIAC! YOU'RE GOING TO KILL US ALL!

oh, DON'T BE SUCH A DRAMA QUEEN, BATMAN. LISTEN TO THOSE SOUNDS! WE'RE NOT IN THREE-DIMENSIONAL SPACE ANYMORE, BABY.

WE'RE HURTLING TOWARDS THE FIFTH DIMENSION AND LAUGHING ALL THE WAY!

PANTS!

HOOPN'S

RALPH!

WELL, EVERYONE EXCEPT THAT GUY TURNING *GREEN* OVER THERE.

SUPERMAN!

HURRY, BATMAN... USE THE ALCHEMICAL WAND... IT'S OUR ONLY HOPE OF DEFEATING THEM...

YOU'RE WASTING YOUR TIME, BATMAN. BRAINIAC 84'S FILES SAID THE ALCHEMICAL WAND ONLY WORKS ON *INANIMATE* OBJECTS.

LIKE *KRYPTONITE*?

COAL! HE'S TURNED THE *KRYPTONITE* ROCK INTO *COAL!*

SAXOPHONE!

NICE WORK, BATMAN!

MY PLEASURE!

FRYING!

unnh!

THOSE ICONS MIGHT HAVE GIVEN *OWAC* ACCESS TO THE GREATEST EVIL MINDS OF ALL TIME, BUT IT SEEMS EVEN MUTO COULDN'T BLOCK A GOOD PUNCH IN THE FACE WHEN IT COUNTED.

GREAT GHOSTS OF KRYPTON! WE'RE HERE...

WE'VE REACHED THE FIFTH DIMENSION— *AAARGGH!*

SUPERMAN?

NOT ANYMORE, BAT-GUY! THE SON OF TOMORROW IS BUSY PLAYING HOST TO A CELEBRITY GUEST! A PEANUT-SIZED BRAIN IN THE ULTIMATE SUPER-HUMAN BODY! THE SMILES OF A UNIVERSE END...

...TONIGHT.

HEY, WHAT'S THE BIG IDEA?

NEVER POSSESS A MAN WITH TEN SENSES MORE THAN YOU HAVE, FRIEND. HE'S ALWAYS GOING TO BE ONE STEP AHEAD.

HOLY DISEMBODIED SPIRIT TRAPPED IN A PSYCHIC BUBBLE OF YOUR OWN CREATION! THE GOOD GUYS WON AGAIN!

HUH? IDENTIFY YOURSELF!

87

SUPER-MITE AND BAT-MITE! YOUR BIGGEST FANS IN THIS REALITY, FELLAS! THE FIFTH DIMENSION'S FINEST SUPER-IMP TEAM!

I WAS WORKING UNDER-COVER AS THE VARANIA WHILE BAT-MITE HERE WAS KEEPING WATCH DISGUISED AS YOUR ENTIRE GALAXY, BUT IT LOOKS LIKE YOU GUYS HAD EVERYTHING UNDER CONTROL AS USUAL...

...I GUESS ALL WE CAN DO NOW IS OFFER YOU A RIDE HOME.

CHWEESE!

PLUTO'S CORE, THE BATCAVE:

THE REVENGE SQUAD'S BACK WHERE THEY BELONG, AND OUR VOWEL-TRADING GENIES STRIPPED OF TWO DIMENSIONS. ALL THINGS CONSIDERED, I'D SAY WE MAKE A PRETTY EFFECTIVE COMBINATION, SUPERMAN.

WATCH OUT, SUPES. I THINK BATMAN'S GONNA ASK YOU OUT ON A DATE...

IT'S A BIG UNIVERSE OUT THERE, BATMAN. MAYBE IT'S TIME THEY HAD A COUPLE OF SUPER-HEROES TEAMING UP TO WATCH OVER THEM AGAIN.

ANYTHING LESS THAN THE BEST WOULD BE UNACCEPTABLE, SUPERMAN.

...LET'S GIVE THEM THE SYSTEM'S FINEST!

THE END!

88

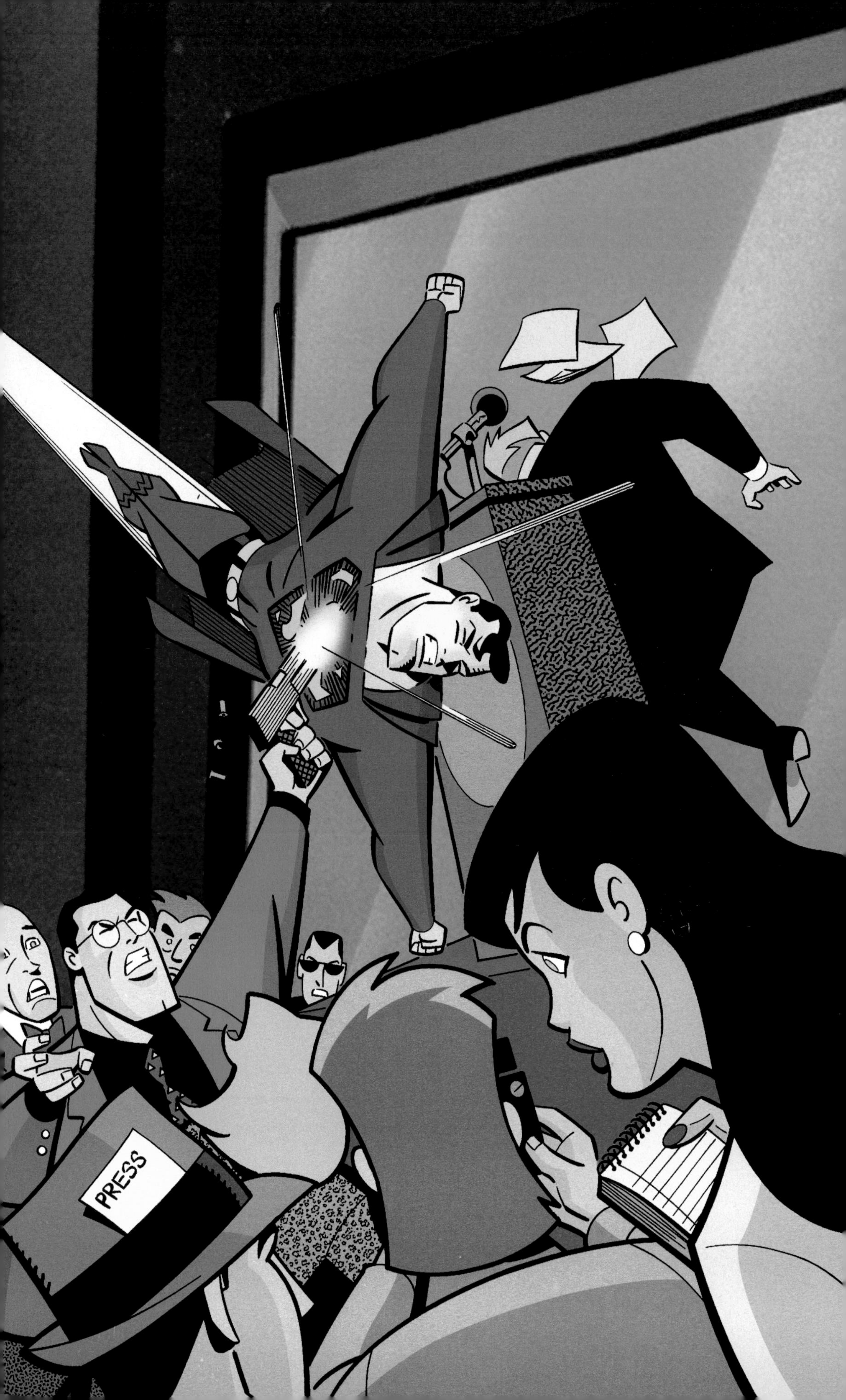
PRESS

THE BODYGUARD OF STEEL

"DON'T WORRY, MISTER PRESIDENT. THIS IS AS CLOSE AS SUPERMAN *GETS* TO THE WHITE HOUSE..."

MARK MILLAR — WRITER
ALUIR AMANCIO — PENCILLER
TERRY AUSTIN — INKER
RICK TAYLOR — COLORIST
LOIS BUHALIS — LETTERER
FRANK BERRIOS — ASSISTANT
MIKE McAVENNIE — EDITOR

SUPERMAN CREATED BY JERRY SIEGEL & JOE SHUSTER

"OUR BOYS HAVE ENOUGH FIREPOWER OUT THERE TO LEVEL THE *STATE*. I PROMISE HE WON'T GET ANYWHERE *NEAR US*."

"THAT'S NOT HOW THINGS LOOK FROM WHERE *I'M* SITTING, GENERAL HARDCASTLE..."

WHOOOOOMM!!

"THE LEXCORP GROUND-TO-AIR MISSILE SYSTEM WAS ONLY OUR *FIRST* LINE OF DEFENSE, SIR. THE ENTIRE BUILDING IS SURROUNDED BY HIGHLY-DECORATED *NAVY SEALS*..."

FWOOSH! FWOOSH!

"THIS IS *DEFINITELY* AS FAR AS HE GOES..."

"...EVEN IF HE MANAGES TO GET PAST THEM, THE NEW WHITE HOUSE EXTERIOR WE DESIGNED IS STRONG ENOUGH TO WITHSTAND THE EFFECTS OF A LOCALIZED *NUCLEAR BLAST*.

RRUMBLE KRAKARAKK

"HE'S STILL COMING, GENERAL. SUPERMAN'S *LIQUIDIZING* YOUR LATEST HARDWARE JUST BY *LOOKING* AT IT..."

"THE CHEMICAL WEAPONS, THE LASER TRIP-WIRE... EVEN THE FREEZER-BLASTS AREN'T BREAKING HIS STRIDE. HE MUST BE TWENTY FEET FROM THE OVAL OFFICE!"

"WHAT ARE WE GOING TO *DO?*"

"*TRUST* ME, MISTER PRESIDENT..."

"...THE NEW ANTI-SUPERHUMAN BARRIER WE HAD INSTALLED OUTSIDE IS TEN FEET THICK AND SOLID TITANIUM.

"EVEN *SUPERMAN* ISN'T GOING TO GET HALFWAY THROUGH THIS BEFORE EVERY MILITARY SERVICEMAN IN THE UNITED STATES PARA-CHUTES ONTO THE WHITE HOUSE LAWN..."

WE'VE GOT MORE THAN ENOUGH TIME TO GET YOU OUT OF HERE IN OUR SPECIALLY-DESIGNED ESCAPE POD.

Uh, GENERAL...

I STILL SAY WE SHOULD'VE MADE MORE OF AN EFFORT TO LOCATE A DECENT PIECE OF KRYPTONITE, BUT THE SITUATION IS NOT UNSATISFACTORY, MISTER PRESIDENT.

...SUPERMAN JUST DISAPPEARED FROM THE SCREEN.

WHAT?!

SECTOR

HE'S IN!

THRUMM

BANG, MISTER PRESIDENT.

YOU'RE DEAD.

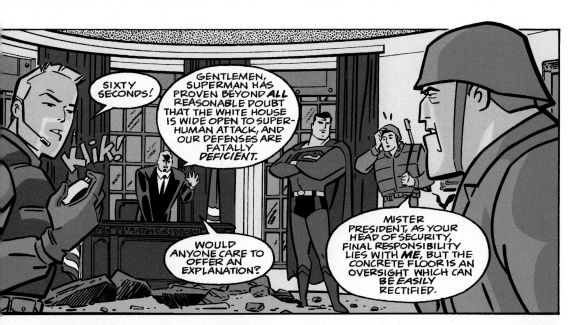

SIXTY SECONDS!

GENTLEMEN, SUPERMAN HAS PROVEN BEYOND *ALL* REASONABLE DOUBT THAT THE WHITE HOUSE IS WIDE OPEN TO SUPER-HUMAN ATTACK, AND OUR DEFENSES ARE FATALLY *DEFICIENT.*

WOULD ANYONE CARE TO OFFER AN EXPLANATION?

MISTER PRESIDENT, AS YOUR HEAD OF SECURITY, FINAL RESPONSIBILITY LIES WITH *ME*, BUT THE CONCRETE FLOOR IS AN OVERSIGHT WHICH CAN BE *EASILY* RECTIFIED.

YOU *KNOW* THE SITUATION, GENERAL-- TIME IS A LUXURY WE CAN'T *AFFORD.*

A PRICE OF *ONE BILLION DOLLARS* HAS BEEN PLACED ON MY HEAD TO STOP ME FROM SIGNING AN INTERNATIONAL PEACE TREATY LESS THAN FORTY-EIGHT HOURS FROM NOW.

OBVIOUSLY, MY OWN SAFETY MEANS *NOTHING*, BUT THE LIVES OF MILLIONS OF PEOPLE THROUGHOUT THE WORLD DEPEND UPON MY SIGNATURE ON THAT PIECE OF PAPER.

I *REFUSE* TO LET SOME TWO-BIT *ASSASSIN* JEOPARDIZE EVEN THE *POSSIBILITY* OF GLOBAL PEACE.

HAVE YOU ANY IDEA WHO'S *OFFERING* THE MONEY, SIR?

THE TRUTH IS THAT IT COULD BE ANY ONE OF A *NUMBER* OF WEAPONS MANUFACTURERS, SUPERMAN.

SEVERAL POWERFUL ORGANIZATIONS THROUGHOUT THE WORLD STAND TO TAKE A SHARP DIP IN PROFITS IF THIS TREATY IS SIGNED, AND THERE'S NO SHORTAGE OF *SUPER-CRIMINALS* WILLING TO CLAIM THE BILLION-DOLLAR REWARD.

THEN I FEEL IT'S MY DUTY TO OFFER MYSELF AS YOUR PERSONAL *BODYGUARD*, MISTER PRESIDENT. AT LEAST UNTIL THE *ASSASSINATION* THREAT HAS BEEN NEUTRALIZED.

THAT'S VERY *GENEROUS* OF YOU, SUPERMAN.

ARE YOU SURE LIVING IN THE WHITE HOUSE TWENTY-FOUR HOURS A DAY WON'T BE AN *INCONVENIENCE*?

OH, GREAT. WE *LOVE* WORKING WITH ALIENS.

WELL, THERE *ARE* ONE OR TWO LITTLE DETAILS I MIGHT HAVE TO TAKE CARE OF *FIRST*...

96

WHAT DO YOU *MEAN* YOU NEED A *VACATION,* KENT?

ONLY FOR A COUPLE OF DAYS, CHIEF.

I COMPLETELY FORGOT ABOUT MY *HIGH SCHOOL REUNION.* LOIS SAID SHE'D BE *MORE* THAN HAPPY TO COVER THAT PEACE TREATY ASSIGNMENT WHILE I'M GONE.

WELL, I DON'T LIKE SHUFFLING MY REPORTERS LIKE A DECK OF *CARDS,* BUT IF LANE RECKONS SHE CAN FIT THIS INTO HER SCHEDULE, I GUESS IT'S OKAY... JUST THIS ONCE.

THANKS, PERRY.

WHAT DO YOU THINK, JIMMY? SMALLVILLE SEEMS A LITTLE *TOO* EAGER TO GET TIME OFF WORK FOR A *SQUARE DANCE.*

I'VE GOT A HUNCH THERE'S SOMETHING THE FARM-BOY'S NOT *TELLING* US HERE.

CAREFUL, LOIS... ...YOU ALMOST SOUNDED *JEALOUS* FOR A MOMENT.

GOOD MORNING, WAGE-SLAVES!

ISN'T IT A *BEAUTIFUL* DAY?

MISTER *LUTHOR?*

WHAT DO THE BOYS CALL *YOU,* GORGEOUS?

Uh, JULIA, SIR. JULIA SCHWARTZ.

LISTEN, JULIA. GET THAT WIG DELOUSED, AND YOU *COULD* BE THE WOMAN WHO GETS LEX LUTHOR TO THE ALTAR.

B-BUT I'M *ALREADY* MARRIED!

Oh, WELL. NO GREAT LOSS.

HOW MUCH DO I PAY YOU FOR SPILLING THAT COFFEE, KID?

Uh...

BUMP!

NEVER MIND. *DOUBLE* IT! YOU'RE WORTH EVERY PENNY!

IN FACT, *EVERYBODY* DOUBLE THEIR WAGES AND TAKE THE REST OF THE DAY OFF... EXCEPT *YOU,* YOUNG MAN.

TAKE ME TO MY PENTHOUSE *IMMEDIATELY.*

98

I DON'T KNOW WHO YOU THINK YOU'RE FOOLING, MISTER, BUT YOU'D BETTER LEAVE THE BUILDING WHILE I STILL FEEL FRIENDLY ENOUGH TO LET YOU USE THE DOOR.

MERCY, MY DEAR, YOU'RE SO SUSPICIOUS.

HOW COULD AN IMPOSTOR POSSIBLY FAKE A DNA SCAN?

BOSS? I'M SORRY. THOUGHT YOU WERE ALREADY HERE. IT'S JUST THAT I'VE NEVER SEEN YOU QUITE LIKE THIS.

LEX LUTHOR I.D. POSITIVE

DID SUPERMAN GET HIT BY A BOMB OR SOMETHING?

OH, LIGHTEN UP, MERCY.

YOU'RE WAY TOO INTENSE FOR SUCH A CUTE CHICK.

Ta-DAAA!

IMPRESSIVE, OR WHAT?

AM I SUPPOSED TO BE IMPRESSED WATCHING YOU DEMOLISH A CAREFULLY CULTIVATED REPUTATION AMONG MY EMPLOYEES?

EEP!

INCIDENTALLY, THOSE PAY RAISES YOU AWARDED THE LITTLE PEOPLE DOWNSTAIRS WILL BE DEDUCTED FROM YOUR FINAL BILL. I'VE ALREADY DONE THE ARITHMETIC...

99

...MULTI-FACE.

ACTUALLY, LUTHOR, YOU'RE SUPPOSED TO BE IMPRESSED BY THE WAY I BREEZED THROUGH ONE OF THE MOST THOROUGH SECURITY SYSTEMS IN THE WORLD!

ARE WE IN BUSINESS HERE, OR AM I WASTING MY TIME?

LET'S START AGAIN, SHALL WE?

MY ASSOCIATES HIRED YOU BECAUSE YOU'RE NOT ONLY A MASTER OF DISGUISE, BUT ONE OF THE WORLD'S GREATEST ASSASSINS. AND I MUST ALWAYS HAVE THE BEST.

PLEASE TAKE A SEAT, MY FRIEND.

LEX, I'D BE DELIGHTED!

WE'VE ALREADY AGREED ON A PRICE, BUT THE ACTUAL TERMS OF THE ASSASSINATION ARE STILL OPEN TO NEGOTIATION.

MY ONLY SPECIFICATION IS THAT A WEAPON OF MY OWN DESIGN IS USED FOR THE KILL...

IT'S REMARKABLY PRECISE AND... HOW SHOULD I PUT IT?... MOVES FASTER THAN YOUR AVERAGE SPEEDING BULLET.

NOTHING ELSE WILL DO THE JOB TO MY SATISFACTION.

100

ICING A GUY LIKE HIM IS GONNA LEAVE A LOT OF GLOOMY PEOPLE OUT THERE, LUTHOR.

I *KNOW.* I'VE KILLED BIG-SHOTS BEFORE.

NONSENSE.

THEY'LL SIMPLY CHOOSE *ANOTHER* AS THEIR FIGUREHEAD, AND HE'LL BE REDUCED TO NOTHING MORE THAN A CHEAP TABLOID CONSPIRACY FOR THE SUPERMARKET CLASSES.

BESIDES, THE TEMPORARY GRIEF OF THE NATION IS OF NO CONSEQUENCE WHEN YOU OPERATE AT *MY* LEVEL.

THIS MURDER IS MERELY A TACTICAL BUSINESS DECISION...

Shhh! YOU HEAR THAT *WHISTLING* SOUND OUTSIDE?

LEXCORP

WALLS HAVE *EARS* IN THIS CITY, LUTHOR, OLD PAL.

CLOSE ONE.

101

LARRY LIEBOWSKI, INDUSTRIAL ASSASSIN ALSO KNOWN AS *MULTI-FACE*, ALSO KNOWN AS ANYONE HE WANTS TO DISGUISE HIMSELF AS.

DESCRIBING HIM AS THE MAN OF A THOUSAND FACES DOESN'T *BEGIN* TO DO THIS GUY JUSTICE, SUPERMAN.

MULTI-FACE CAN ASSUME THE VOICE, POSTURE AND CREATE THE FEATURES OF ANYONE HE DESIRES. HE ALSO HAS THE ABILITY TO FOOL EVEN THE MOST SOPHISTICATED X-RAYS.

FBI SOURCES RECKON MULTI-FACE HAS BEEN HIRED TO CARRY OUT THE BIGGEST HIT OF HIS CAREER. THE BAD NEWS IS THAT HE'S NEVER MISSED A TARGET YET.

KLIK!

ANY QUESTIONS?

ONLY *ONE*, GENERAL HARDCASTLE.

WHY DON'T YOU LIKE HAVING ME AROUND THE WHITE HOUSE?

I'VE NEVER MADE ANY SECRET OF THE FACT THAT I'M UNCOMFORTABLE AROUND *ALIENS,* SUPERMAN.

AS I'VE TOLD YOU BEFORE, I DON'T TRUST WHAT I CAN'T CONTROL, AND I DON'T LIKE WHAT I CAN'T TRUST.

IS THAT SUPPOSED TO BE A HINT YOU'D RATHER I WASN'T *INVOLVED* IN THIS CASE, GENERAL HARDCASTLE?

THINGS MIGHT BE DIFFERENT IF YOU OPERATED UNDER THE INSTRUCTIONS OF THE U.S. GOVERNMENT, BUT YOU'VE ALWAYS MADE IT CLEAR YOU WON'T BECOME INVOLVED IN MILITARY MATTERS, AND THAT MAKES ME HIGHLY SUSPICIOUS.

BUT WHAT REALLY ANNOYS ME, WHAT REALLY TICKS ME OFF, IS THAT THE REAL HEROES OUT THERE ON THE FRONT LINES DON'T GET ANY RECOGNITION SINCE *YOU* APPEARED, FLYBOY.

ANYONE CAN BE THE MAIN MAN WHEN BULLETS BOUNCE OFF THEIR CHEST INSTEAD OF PASSING STRAIGHT THROUGH.

AAAA!

WHICH WAY TO THE OVAL OFFICE?

TOYMAN HAS A DELIVERY FOR THE PRESIDENT!

VROOSH!

VROOSH!

VROOSH!

103

TOYMAN, YOU MANIAC! WHAT DO YOU THINK YOU'RE DOING?!

BOOM!

KABOOM!

KaBOOM!

SKRUNCH!

TRYING TO EARN A BILLION DOLLARS BY REMOTE CONTROL FROM A SECRET LOCATION, SUPERMAN. WHAT DO YOU THINK?

BY THE WAY, THIS CHILDHOOD FAVORITE IS CARRYING A HIROSHIMA SPECIAL SET TO DETONATE IN TEN SECONDS...

...FOUR OF WHICH HAVE ALREADY PASSED.

WHAT DID HE SAY, SUPERMAN?

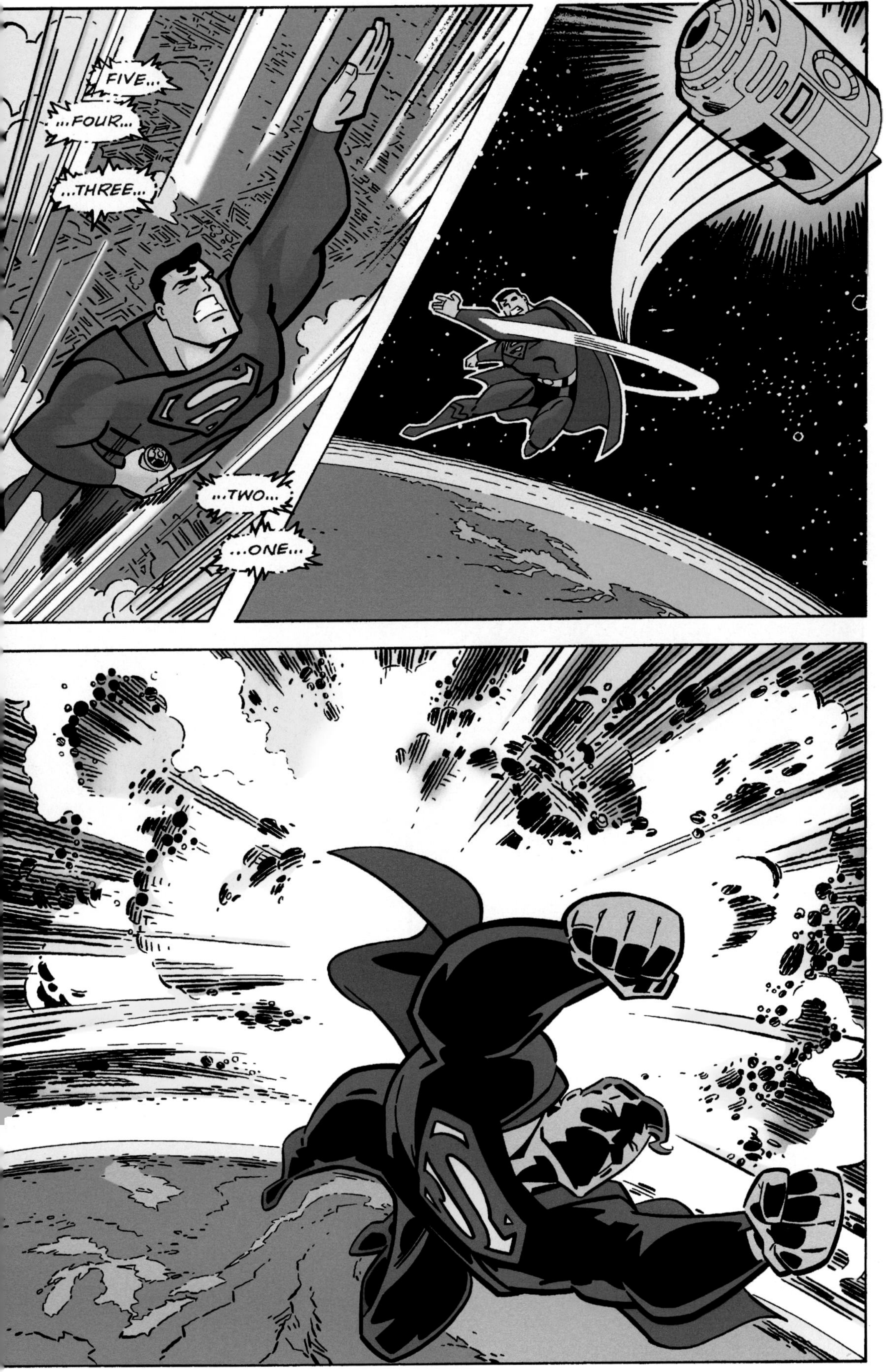

FIVE...
...FOUR...
...THREE...
...TWO...
...ONE...

"THE PARASITE, METALLO, MEMBERS OF INTERGANG, AND THE WEATHER WIZARD HAVE ALL KEPT SUPERMAN BUSY ON HIS SECOND DAY AT THE WHITE HOUSE IN A SERIES OF BIZARRE ASSASSINATION ATTEMPT...

"...BUT A CASH-STRAPPED TOYMAN, WITH HIS ARMY OF KILLER ROBOTS, HAS BEEN, PERHAPS, THE MOST EAGER TO CLAIM THE BILLION DOLLARS IN BLOOD MONEY."

SSKKRAASSHH!

SUPERMAN! TAKE A FEW MOMENTS TO EXPLAIN HOW SOMEONE ACTUALLY DEFEATS A FIFTY-FOOT-TALL TOY INTENT ON TRAMPLING THE WHITE HOUSE INTO THE DIRT?

CERTAINLY, MISS...

YOU TAKE OUT THE BATTERIES?!

YOU *DID* ASK.

CONTROL, WE'VE GOT A MISS LANE HERE FROM THE DAILY PLANET SEEKING ACCESS TO THE PRESS SECTION. I CAN'T FIND HER NAME ON ANY OF THE LISTS.

NO NAME MEANS NO AUTHORIZATION, SECURITY FOUR. WE CAN'T BEND THE RULES FOR ANYONE WHEN THE PRESIDENT IS THIS CLOSE TO SIGNING THE PEACE TREATY.

SORRY, MISS LANE. I'M AFRAID I'M GOING TO HAVE TO ASK YOU TO LEAVE THE PREMISES.

THIS IS INSANE! FIRST THE HOTEL IS STILL BOOKED IN CLARK KENT'S NAME, AND NOW I CAN'T EVEN GET INTO THE STUPID PRESS CONFERENCE!

ALLOW ME TO ESCORT YOU, LOIS. I ALWAYS BOOK AN EXTRA SEAT IN CASE I FIND A DAMSEL IN DISTRESS.

FRANKLY, I DIDN'T THINK A PEACE SUMMIT WAS A TYPICAL NIGHT OUT FOR A NOTORIOUS WEAPONS MANUFACTURER LIKE YOU, LEX LUTHOR.

AS EVER, MY DEAR, YOU COMPLETELY MISJUDGE ME.

I WOULDN'T MISS THIS FOR THE WORLD.

107

SUPERMAN, THIS IS GENERAL HARDCASTLE.

OUR INTELLIGENCE BOYS HAVE JUST CONFIRMED MULTI-FACE STILL PLANS TO GO AHEAD WITH THE ASSASSINATION.

THESE ARE THE SAME BOYS WHO TOLD US MULTI-FACE HAD BEEN HIRED FOR THE JOB, SUPERMAN. YOU CAN TRUST THESE SOLDIERS WITH YOUR LIFE.

ARE YOU SURE ABOUT THIS, GENERAL?

X-RAY ANALYSIS DOESN'T SUGGEST ANYTHING OUT OF THE ORDINARY DOWN THERE...

THAT'S BECAUSE MULTI-FACE CAN CONFUSE ALL KINDS OF DETECTION. WE JUST HAVE TO WAIT FOR HIM TO MAKE HIS MOVE AND HOPE YOU'RE AS FAST AS YOU SAY YOU ARE.

LADIES AND GENTLEMEN, THE PRESIDENT OF THE UNITED STATES OF AMERICA...

WAIT A MINUTE, GENERAL.

I THINK I'VE GOT SOMETHING.

I DON'T BELIEVE THIS.

WHAT IS IT, SUPERMAN? WHAT'S WRONG?

TALK ABOUT THE WRONG FACE AT THE WRONG TIME.

WOULD THE GENTLEMAN DISGUISED AS THE DAILY PLANET REPORTER IN THE THIRD ROW PLEASE STAND UP AND REMOVE HIS MASK?

HOW IN THE NAME OF...?

WHAT IS IT, SOLDIER? SUPERMAN'S JUST CAUGHT MULTI-FACE OUT THERE!

GENERAL, I THINK THERE'S SOMETHING YOU SHOULD KNOW...

YOU IDIOTIC *LUNK!* DO YOU REALLY THINK THIS INTERVENTION IS GOING TO *DIVERT* ME FROM MY MISSION FOR A SECOND?

READ THE PAPERS, MULTI-FACE. BULLETS TEND TO BOUNCE *OFF* MY CHEST, BUT YOU'RE WELCOME TO *TRY.*

SUPERMAN, GET OUT OF THE WAY!

YOU'RE THE ONE HE WAS HIRED TO *KILL!*

SHUT UP!

CH'OOOM!

110

MULTI-FACE NEVER PLANNED TO MURDER THE *PRESIDENT* AT ALL! *YOU* WERE HIS TARGET RIGHT FROM THE START!

THANK YOU, GENERAL. LET'S JUST MAKE SURE HE DOESN'T GET A *SECOND* CHANCE...

GREAT...

EXCUSE ME, BUSTER...

...I THINK YOU'RE SITTING IN *MY SEAT!*

KLUNNK!

EVER THOUGHT OF A CAREER AS A *BODYGUARD,* LOIS?

DAILY PLANET

SECURITY SERVICE FOILS PLOT TO KILL SUPERMAN

EXCLUSIVE BY LOIS LANE

TYPICAL OF SUPERMAN TO BE SO CONCERNED ABOUT SOMEONE ELSE, HE DIDN'T REALIZE HE WAS THE ONE MULTI-FACE WAS AIMING FOR WITH THAT HIGH-IMPACT BLASTER.

AND TO THINK THE SCOOP COULD HAVE BEEN YOURS IF YOU HADN'T OPTED FOR THE SQUARE DANCE, KENT.

ALL'S FAIR IN LOVE AND PRINT JOURNALISM, LOIS.

DAILY PLANET
SECURITY SERVICES FOILS PLOT TO KILL SUPERM

KENT, STOP TALKING AND START TYPING! TWO DAYS' VACATION MEANS YOU HAVE TO WORK TWICE AS HARD WHEN YOU GET BACK, AND I DON'T WANT TO HEAR ANY EXCUSES!

WOW. WELCOME BACK, huh?

WAIT A MINUTE! THIS DOESN'T MAKE ANY SENSE...

IF MULTI-FACE WAS HIRED AS AN ASSASSIN, WHY DID HE AIM FOR SUPERMAN WHEN HE COULD HAVE TAKEN A SHOT AT THE PRESIDENT AND EARNED HIMSELF A BILLION DOLLARS?!

I DIDN'T KNOW HE WAS THAT PATRIOTIC.

SMALL

UNFORTUNATELY, HE'S NOT, JIMMY. WORD IS HE WAS OFFERED TWO BILLION DOLLARS TO GET RID OF SUPERMAN.

I JUST HOPE THE PRESIDENT DOESN'T TAKE IT PERSONALLY.

THE END

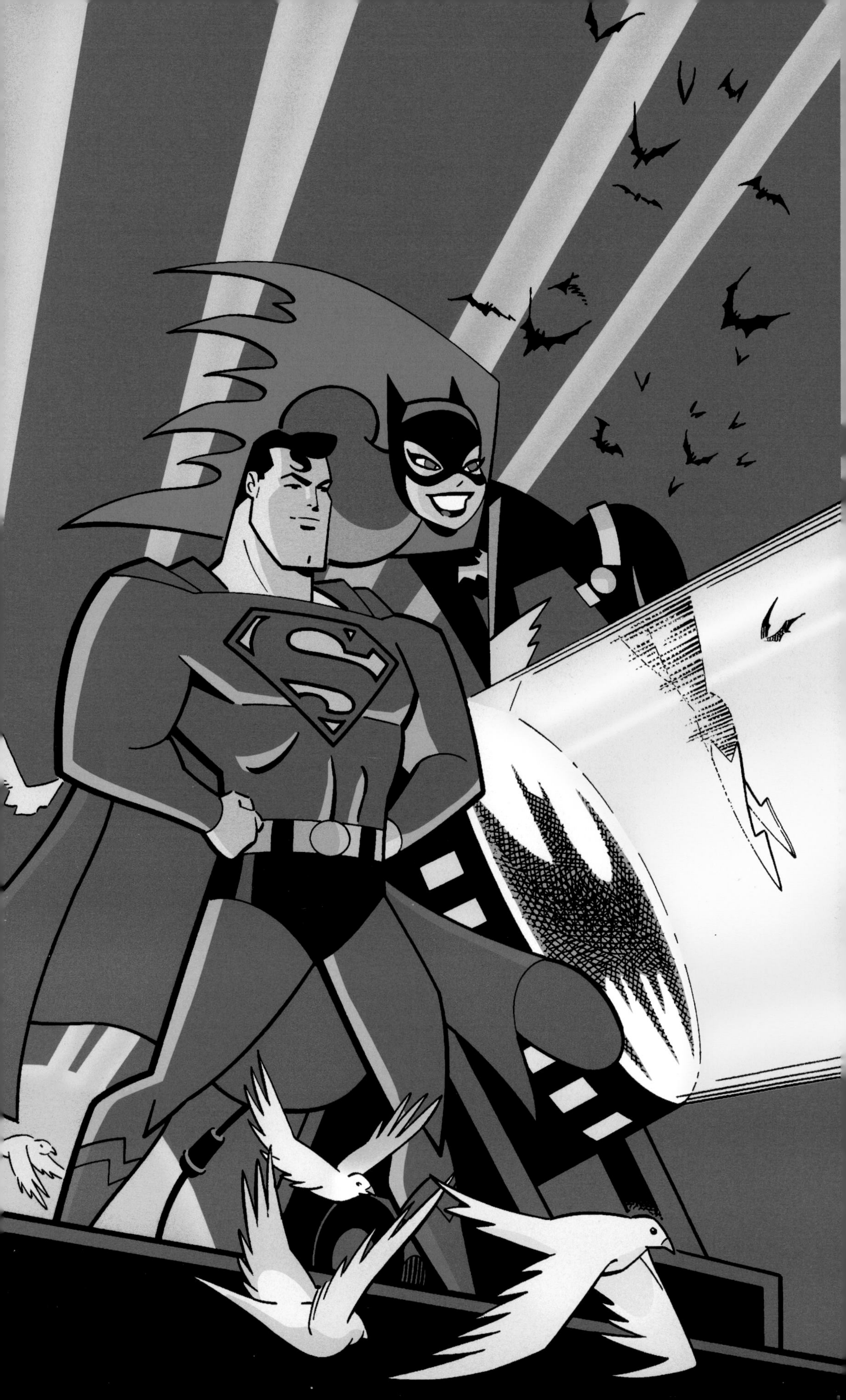

(Almost) The World's Finest Team

BATMAN! YOU HAVE UNTIL *MIDNIGHT* TO SURRENDER YOUR COWL ON *LIVE TELEVISION*, OR BILLIONAIRE *BRUCE WAYNE* DROPS A COUPLE OF HAT SIZES!

WHAT IS IT TO *BE*, OLD BOY?

MARK MILLAR - WRITER
MIKE MANLEY - PENCILLER
TERRY AUSTIN - INKER
MARIE SEVERIN - COLORIST
ZYLONOL - SEPARATIONS
LOIS BUHALIS - LETTERER
FRANK BERRIOS - ASSISTANT EDITOR
MIKE McAVENNIE - EDITOR

SUPERMAN CREATED BY JERRY SIEGEL & JOE SHUSTER

BATMAN CREATED BY BOB KANE

115

THE MAD HATTER GOT BRUCE?

SLEEPING PILLS IN HIS *TUNA CARPACCIO,* AT THE GOTHAM ORPHANAGE BENEFIT LUNCHEON, MASTER NIGHTWING. WE NEED YOU BACK HOME IMMEDIATELY.

BUT I'VE ONLY JUST WRAPPED UP THE *KILLER CROC JAILBREAK,* ALFRED. EVEN IF I *CHARTERED* A PLANE RIGHT NOW, I WOULDN'T MAKE LOUISIANA TO GOTHAM BY *TWELVE.*

WHAT ABOUT ROBIN OR BATGIRL?

I'M AFRAID THAT'S OUR SECOND PROBLEM, YOUNG SIR. MASTER TIMOTHY IS IN UNIFORM, BUT I'VE LOST ALL COMMUNICATION WITH HIM.

IF OUR LUCK SO FAR THIS EVENING IS ANYTHING TO *JUDGE* BY, I WOULD SAY THAT'S A RELATIVELY *SAFE* ASSUMPTION.

BATGIRL AND I ARE BECOMING VERY CONCERNED.

LT88

THE HATTER?

116

YOU KNOW, BATMAN, I'M THE *FIRST* TO ADMIT, THERE IS A CERTAIN SADISM IN MY ACTIONS HERE TONIGHT...

...*AFTER ALL*, THIS CEREMONIAL UNMASKING *COULD* HAVE BEEN A *DIGNIFIED* AFFAIR, FAR FROM THE PUBLIC GAZE. INSTEAD, I'VE OPTED TO PRODUCE THE TV RATINGS *BONANZA* OF THE CENTURY...

...WHERE I COMPLETE MY *COLLECTION* OF UNIQUE HEAD GARMENTS, AND GOTHAM CITY DISCOVERS *YOUR SECRET IDENTITY.*

Oh, AND DON'T EXPECT TO BE BAILED OUT BY ANY OF YOUR BAT-HELPERS, EITHER. LITTLE ROBIN TRIED AND FAILED, BUT THAT'S WHAT HAPPENS WHEN YOU SEND A BOY TO DO A *BATMAN'S* JOB.

TICK-TOCK, TICK-TOCK.

TIME IS RUNNING OUT FOR BRUCE WAYNE, CAPED CRUSADER.

IS YOUR SECRET IDENTITY REALLY *MORE IMPORTANT* THAN THE LIFE OF GOTHAM'S GREATEST HUMANITARIAN? SAY IT ISN'T SO!

NO SIGN OF HIM, COMMISH. MAYBE BATMAN'S WATCHIN' CABLE OR SOMETHIN' AND *MISSED* THE WHOLE SHOW.

OR MAYBE THAT SECRET IDENTITY OF HIS *IS* MORE IMPORTANT TO HIM THAN SOME *WELL-HEELED PLAYBOY* HE'S NEVER EVEN MET.

ABSOLUTELY NOT, SERGEANT BULLOCK. HIS METHODS MAY BE A LITTLE *UNORTHODOX* SOMETIMES, BUT BATMAN VALUES NOTHING MORE THAN HUMAN LIFE.

MARK MY WORDS, HE'LL BE HERE.

I'M SURE HE'D APPRECIATE THE VOTE OF CONFIDENCE, COMMISSIONER.

BATMAN'S ON A CASE OUT OF TOWN, SIR, BUT I CAUGHT THE HATTER'S BROADCAST ON TV.

MIND IF I LEND A HAND?

BATMAN...?

GOOD LORD, NO. IT'S A PLEASURE TO FINALLY *MEET* YOU, SUPERMAN. I'VE BEEN FOLLOWING YOUR CAREER SINCE YOU FIRST APPEARED. BATMAN HOLDS YOU IN THE HIGHEST REGARD.

ACTUALLY, I WONDERED IF YOU KNEW *WHY* THE HATTER NEVER SAID WHERE HE WAS IF HE'S SO DESPERATE FOR BATMAN TO FIND HIM.

THE CLOCK'S *TICKIN'*, COMMISH.

'CAUSE HE FIGURES *ONLY BATS* HAS WHAT IT TAKES TO HUNT HIM DOWN WITH ZERO CLUES. PRETTY SMART, *huh?*

YOU'RE DEALING WITH A DIFFERENT TYPE OF CRIMINAL NOW, SUPERMAN. *GOTHAM CITY* IS NO METROP-OLIS.

PEOPLE HERE ARE *TOO SCARED* TO LOOK UP IN THE SKIES...

...AND BELIEVE ME, THEY HAVE...

Uh, COMMISH...? HE'S GONE.

≳Sigh≲ WHAT *IS* IT WITH THESE PEOPLE?

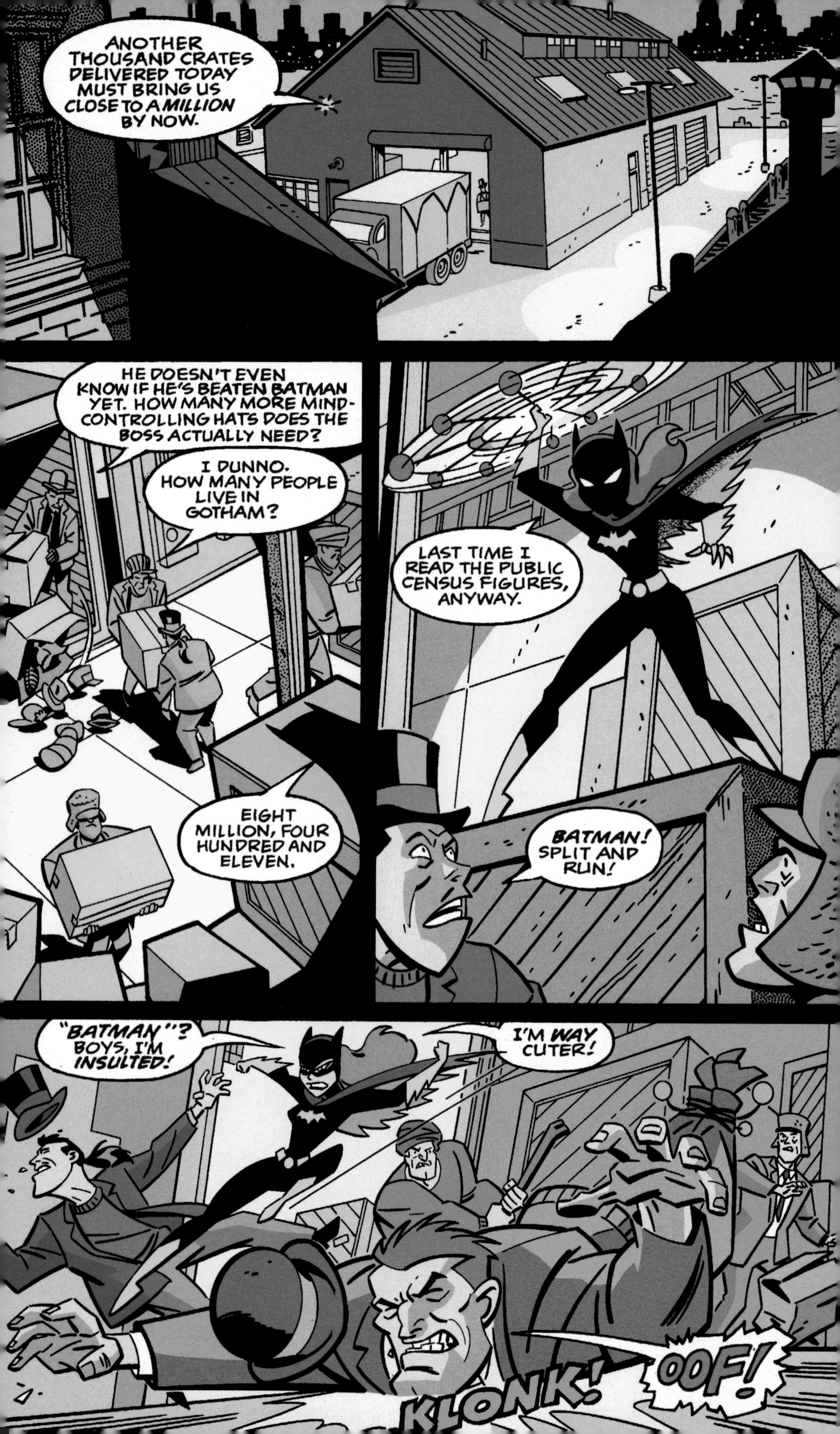
ANOTHER THOUSAND CRATES DELIVERED TODAY MUST BRING US CLOSE TO A *MILLION* BY NOW.
HE DOESN'T EVEN KNOW IF HE'S BEATEN BATMAN YET. HOW MANY MORE MIND-CONTROLLING HATS DOES THE BOSS ACTUALLY NEED?
I DUNNO. HOW MANY PEOPLE LIVE IN GOTHAM?
EIGHT MILLION, FOUR HUNDRED AND ELEVEN.
LAST TIME I READ THE PUBLIC CENSUS FIGURES, ANYWAY.
BATMAN! SPLIT AND RUN!
"*BATMAN*"? BOYS, I'M *INSULTED!*
I'M *WAY* CUTER!
KLONK!
OOF!

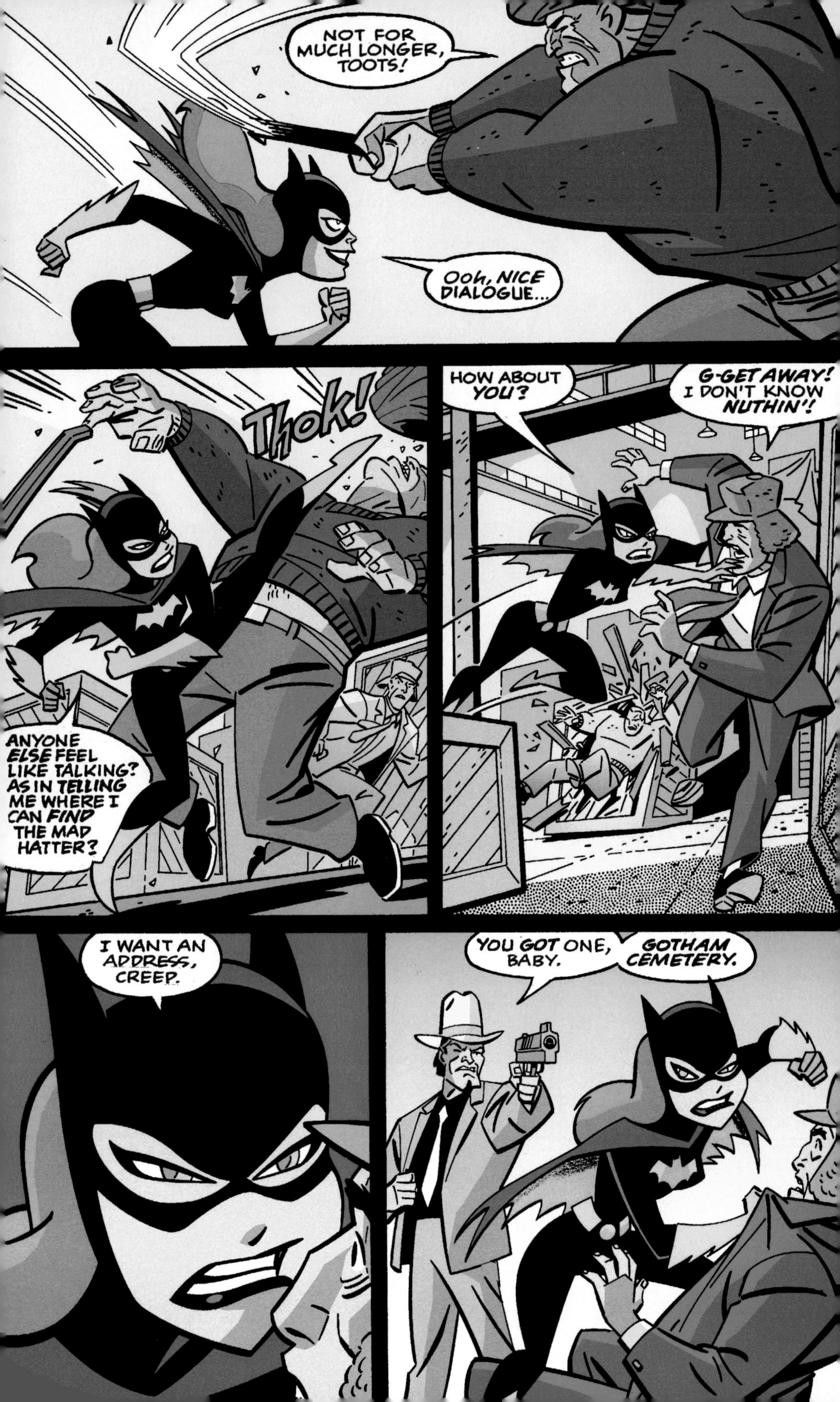
NOT FOR MUCH LONGER, TOOTS!
Ooh, NICE DIALOGUE...
THOK!
ANYONE ELSE FEEL LIKE TALKING? AS IN TELLING ME WHERE I CAN FIND THE MAD HATTER?
HOW ABOUT YOU?
G-GET AWAY! I DON'T KNOW NUTHIN'!
I WANT AN ADDRESS, CREEP.
YOU GOT ONE, BABY.
GOTHAM CEMETERY.

LOSE THE GUN, MISTER!

WHOOM!

SUPERMAN-- AAAGHH!

OH, NO...

CONGRATULATIONS. YOU JUST SET US BACK A CRUCIAL TWENTY MINUTES.

EXCUSE ME?

WHAT BAT-CHICK MEANS, SUPERMAN, IS THAT THE *VIOLENTLY PERSUASIVE TACTICS* SHE AND HER FRIENDS EMPLOY *AREN'T* GOING TO WORK ON US SO LONG AS *YOU'RE* AROUND FOR PROTECTION.

WHAT MAKES YOU THINK I'M GOING TO PROTECT *YOU?*

YOU SEE MY FRIENDS BACK THERE...?

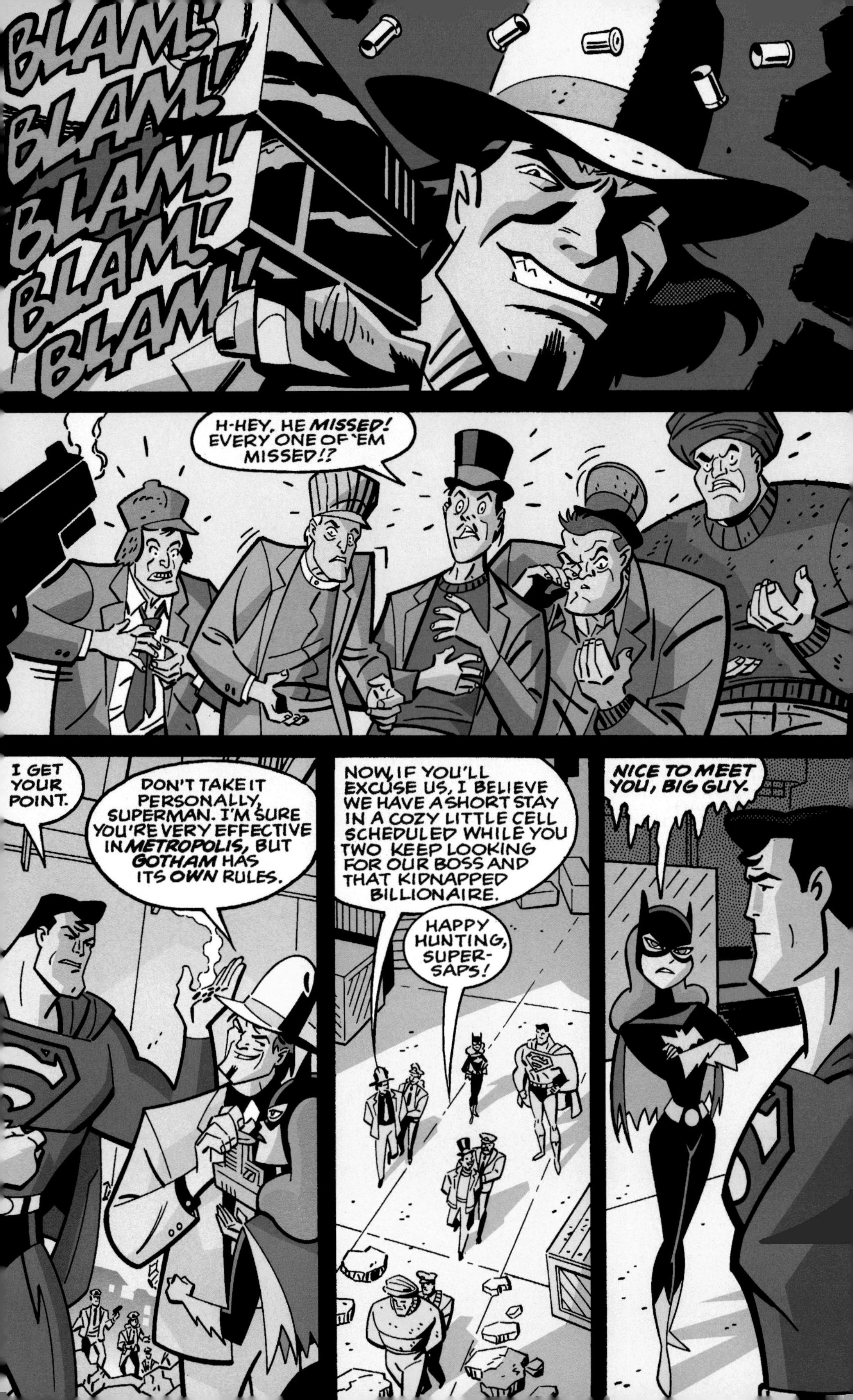
BLAM! BLAM! BLAM! BLAM! BLAM!
H-HEY, HE MISSED! EVERY ONE OF 'EM MISSED!?
I GET YOUR POINT.
DON'T TAKE IT PERSONALLY, SUPERMAN. I'M SURE YOU'RE VERY EFFECTIVE IN METROPOLIS, BUT GOTHAM HAS ITS OWN RULES.
NOW, IF YOU'LL EXCUSE US, I BELIEVE WE HAVE A SHORT STAY IN A COZY LITTLE CELL SCHEDULED WHILE YOU TWO KEEP LOOKING FOR OUR BOSS AND THAT KIDNAPPED BILLIONAIRE.
HAPPY HUNTING, SUPER-SAPS!
NICE TO MEET YOU, BIG GUY.

I'M GUESSING A MAN WITH X-RAY VISION IS UP TO SPEED ON *WHY* THIS BRUCE WAYNE SITUATION IS AN EXTRA-SPECIAL PROBLEM.

I REGARD PEEKING BEHIND MASKS AS AN INVASION OF *PRIVACY*, BUT BATMAN *FORCED* THE ISSUE WHEN I FIRST MET HIM.

JUST DON'T DO IT TO *ME*, BUSTER.

OKAY, OUR NEXT BEST HOPE OF FINDING THE HATTER JUST WALKED OUT OF THE *REFORMED CRIMINALS SOCIETY BAR...*

...JACK MOTEL, A.K.A. "THE REAL ESTATE AGENT OF EVIL." SEEMS THERE ISN'T A SOCIOPATH BREAKS OUT OF ARKHAM WITHOUT ARRANGING THEIR SECRET HIDEOUT THROUGH GOOD OLD JACK FIRST.

LEAVE THIS ONE TO ME.

OKAY, BUT REMEMBER-- YOU'RE IN *GOTHAM*. THINK *"BATMAN."*

I CAN *DO* BATMAN.

GOOD EVENING, JACK. YOU'RE ON THE METROPOLIS TO GOTHAM FLIGHT PATH AT THE MOMENT, AND THERE'S A PLANE SCHEDULED TO CROSS THIS SPOT IN LESS THAN A MINUTE.

WHA—WHAT DO YOU WANT? WHAT DO YOU WANT?

JUST A LITTLE INFORMATION REGARDING THE WHEREABOUTS OF THE MAD HATTER.

I—I SWEAR, SUPERMAN! HE NEVER RENTED FROM ME! HE SAID HE WAS GONNA HOLE UP IN THE LAST PLACE ANYONE'D FIND HIM! HE SAID HE DIDN'T NEED ME!

HERE COMES THAT FLIGHT, JACK...

ON MY MOTHER'S GRAVE! HE NEVER RENTED FROM ME!

TALK FAST, JACK. WE DON'T HAVE MUCH TIME.

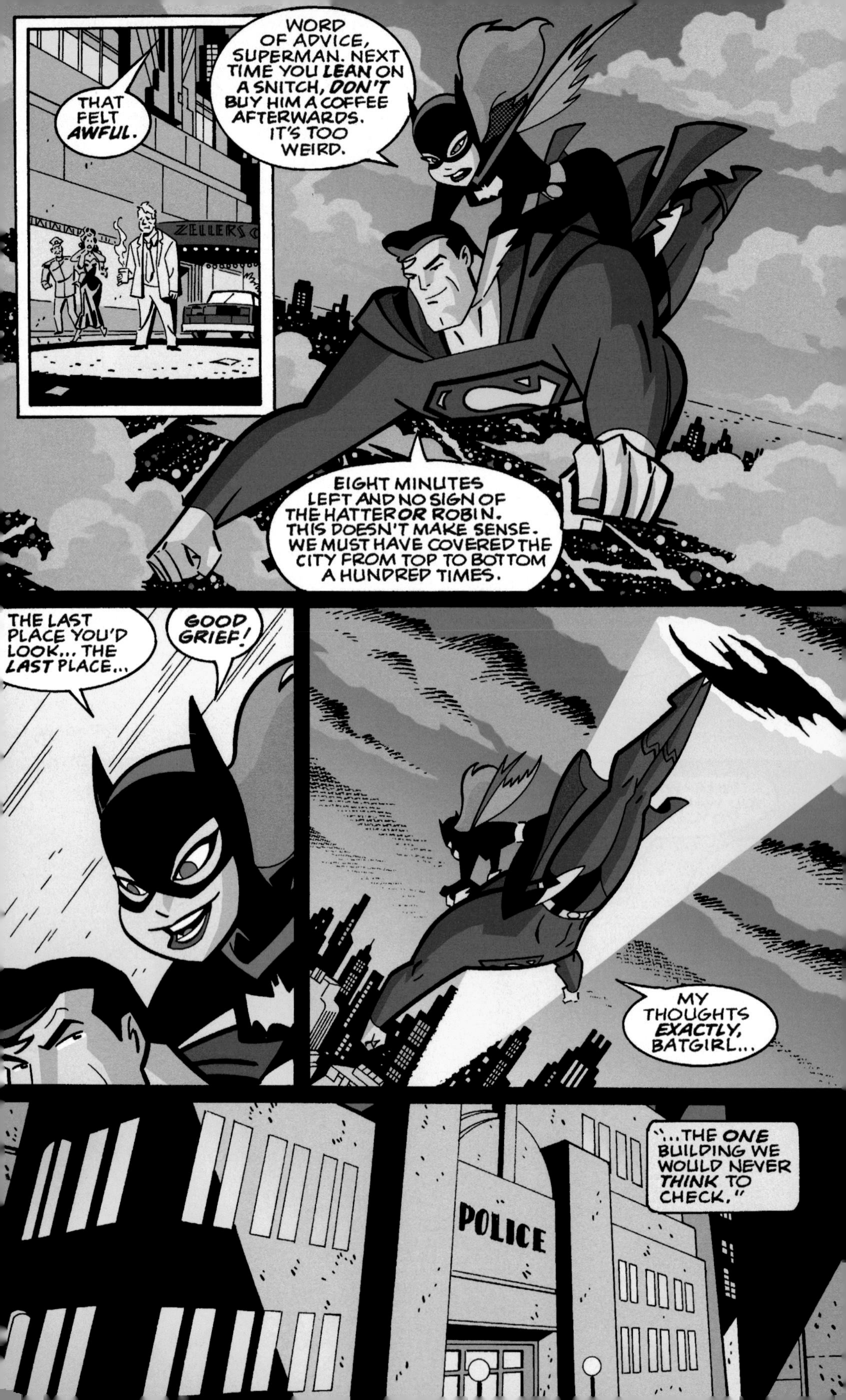
THAT FELT AWFUL.
WORD OF ADVICE, SUPERMAN. NEXT TIME YOU LEAN ON A SNITCH, DON'T BUY HIM A COFFEE AFTERWARDS. IT'S TOO WEIRD.
ZELLERS
EIGHT MINUTES LEFT AND NO SIGN OF THE HATTER OR ROBIN. THIS DOESN'T MAKE SENSE. WE MUST HAVE COVERED THE CITY FROM TOP TO BOTTOM A HUNDRED TIMES.
THE LAST PLACE YOU'D LOOK... THE LAST PLACE...
GOOD GRIEF!
MY THOUGHTS EXACTLY, BATGIRL...
"...THE ONE BUILDING WE WOULD NEVER THINK TO CHECK."
POLICE

CITIZENS OF GOTHAM--I *REGRET* TO REPORT THAT BATMAN HAS CHEATED AND ENLISTED THE HELP OF SOMEONE FROM *WAY* OUT OF TOWN.

THEREFORE, THE RULES OF THE GAME MUST BE CHANGED.

MY *BACKUP PLAN* IS NOW IN ACTION, WHERE ROBIN THE BOY WONDER, WEARING ONE OF MY MIND-CONTROLLING HATS, HAS BEEN COMMANDED TO CREATE A SUPERMAN-SCALE DIVERSION...

...ILLA!

...INVOLVING THE BIGGEST PLANE HE CAN FIND, AND A TARGET YOU CALL THE HEART OF GOTHAM CITY.

CRASH HELMETS AT THE READY, BOYS AND GIRLS...

...I ESTIMATE YOU HAVE *TWO MINUTES.*

OH, YEAH...

LET'S PARTY.

NY LAST WORDS?

HATTER, LISTEN TO ME! THERE'S SOMETHING YOU HAVE TO KNOW...

I'M SORRY, WAYNE, BUT NOTHING YOU CAN SAY OR DO ALTERS THE FACT THAT BATMAN HAS YOUR BLOOD ON HIS HANDS TONIGHT. AND ALL BECAUSE HE WOULDN'T PART WITH A BEAUTIFUL, STUPID COWL.

PUT THE GUN DOWN, HATTER.

I'M SERIOUS.

"BAT-MAN!" I SAID, "BAT-MAN!"

YOU CAN'T POSSIBLY BE SERIOUS, MY DEAR.

TELL THE BOYS TO BLOW HER AWAY, COMMISSIONER!

KEEPING ABREAST OF CURRENT EVENTS WITH YOUR SUPER-HEARING, MAN OF STEEL?

OR ARE YOU OTHERWISE DISTRACTED BY BOY WONDER'S KAMIKAZE MISSION OVER DOWNTOWN GOTHAM? POOR ROBIN CAN'T DISOBEY A SINGLE COMMAND SO LONG AS WE BOTH WEAR THESE HATS!

THAT'S WHY I'M SENDING HIM STRAIGHT TO HADES, AND HE'S TAKING HALF OF GOTHAM WITH HIM!

ROBIN! LISTEN TO ME! YOU HAVE TO CHANGE COURSE OR *THOUSANDS* OF INNOCENT PEOPLE *WILL DIE!*

THERE'S ONLY ONE GUY I LISTEN TO NOW SUPERMAN...

...AND HE DOESN'T WEAR TIGHTS.

NO TIME TO BE GENTLE ABOUT THIS!

AUIGGH!

NOW *PULL UP,* BEFORE IT'S *TOO LATE!*

OKAY, *OKAY!*

ALL *RIGHT,* SUPERMAN!

YOU SHOWED THE MAD HATTER WHO *ROCKS* IN GOTHAM CITY!

HEY, WHAT'S HAPPENING, S-MAN? LAST THING I REMEMBER WAS BEING CLOBBERED BY THE MAD HATTER. DOES BATMAN KNOW I'M FLYING HIS BAT-WING?

NO TIME FOR THE DETAILS, SON...

WHOOP! WHOOP! WHOOP!

ALL I WANTED WAS TO STEAL HIS PRECIOUS COWL, AND HE'S TURNED ME INTO ONE OF THE BIGGEST MASS MURDERERS IN AMERICAN HISTORY.

OH, WOE IS ME...

WELL, WHAT ARE YOU *WAITING* FOR, GORDON? HANUKKAH?

GIVE YOUR MEN THE KILL ORDER!

I ... I CAN'T...

OH, NEVER MIND!

OPEN FIRE ON THE CUTE CRUSADER ON THE COUNT OF THREE, BOYS AND GIRLS.

ONE...

TWO...

GO FOR THE HAT, BATGIRL ...

132

WHACK!

ZZZT!

THREE!

HEY, WHAT THE HECK'S BEEN GOIN' ON HERE?

COMMISSIONER, ARE YOU OKAY?

DON'T WORRY ABOUT ME! JUST GET AFTER HIM!

I'M NOT GOING BACK TO ARKHAM!

THAT PLACE IS FULL OF LUNATICS!

OH, NO, YOU DON'T!

NOBODY GETS AWAY FROM ME THAT EASY!

OOPS.

MAYBE I SHOULD TAKE THAT BACK...

Ploosh!

ANY LUCK?

ONLY THE *BAD* KIND, SUPERMAN.

THE ALLOYS USED IN SEWER PIPING ARE LEAD-BASED, WHICH NIXES YOUR X-RAY VISION...

...AND THE MILES OF TUNNEL DOWN HERE WOULD TAKE HOURS TO SEARCH EVEN WITH YOUR SUPER-SPEED.

GOOD THING I PAID A LITTLE VISIT TO THE BAT-CAVE BEFORE I GOT HERE, AND RAIDED THE WARDROBE.

HEY, CLEVER BOY...

"...ESPECIALLY WHEN OUR QUARRY IS KIND OF *UNDER-DRESSED* IN THE HEAD DEPARTMENT FOR THE FIRST TIME IN HIS LIFE."

BATMAN'S COWL, HATTER.

YOU WERE WILLING TO DO WHATEVER IT TOOK TO ADD THIS TO YOUR COLLECTION, AND HERE IT IS, BEING HANDED TO YOU ON A PLATE.

NO STRINGS ATTACHED.

I CAN'T IMAGINE WHAT YOU'RE GOING THROUGH OUT THERE.

THERE'S NOTHING MORE UNSIGHTLY THAN A HATLESS HEAD, AND THIS COWL IS SUCH A WONDERFUL PIECE OF ENGLISH CRAFTSMAN-SHIP...

YOU'D LOOK TERRIFIC IN IT. YOU REALLY WOULD.

OH, THANK YOU, SUPERMAN.

THANK YOU, THANK YOU, THANK YOU.

MAD AS A HATTER.

NO DOUBT ABOUT IT...

...BUT YOU DON'T HAVE TO BREAK SOMEONE'S RIBS TO SOLVE A CASE, BATGIRL.

INTERESTING IDEA.

THANKS. I ALWAYS APPRECIATE THE HAND.

"THANKS"? HE SAVED OUR LIVES, YOUR SECRET IDENTITY, THOUSANDS OF CIVILIANS, AND BUSTED THE MAD HATTER FOR US, BOSS.

THEREFORE, I THANKED HIM. WHAT'S YOUR POINT, ROBIN?

PERSONALLY, I GET THE FEELING BATMAN DOESN'T APPROVE OF SUPERMAN'S FLAMBOYANT, WIDE-SCREEN TACTICS IN HIS HOMETOWN.

ON THE CONTRARY, BATGIRL...

"...SUPERMAN'S METHODS ARE VERY EFFECTIVE IN THEIR OWN WAY, AND THERE'S NO DENYING GOTHAM SEEMS A LITTLE BRIGHTER FOR HIS PRESENCE.

"I THINK IT DOES US ALL GOOD TO LOOK UP IN THE SKY...

"...EVERY ONCE IN A WHILE."

THE END

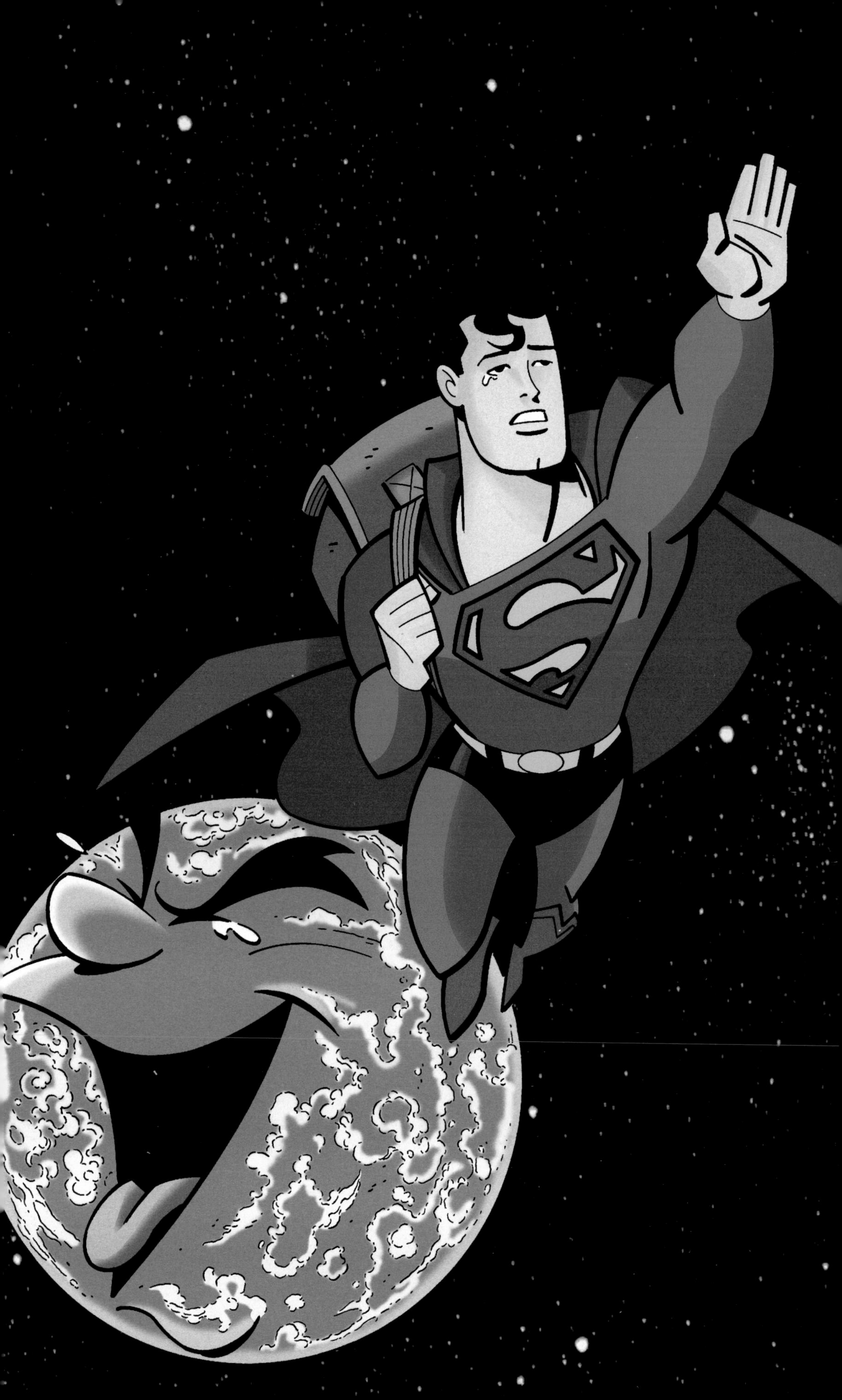

Yesterday's MAN of TOMORROW

AW, *CRIPES!* MY NINETY DAYS ARE ALMOST UP AND I *STILL* DON'T HAVE A PLAN TO BEAT SUPERMAN. WHAT AM I GONNA *DO,* HONEY?

SPEND SOME QUALITY TIME WITH ME INSTEAD?

MARK MILLAR - WRITER
ALUIR AMANCIO - PENCILLER
TERRY AUSTIN - INKER
MARIE SEVERIN - COLORIST
ZYLONOL - SEPS
LOIS BUHALIS - LETTERER
FRANK BERRIOS - ASSISTANT EDITOR
MIKE McAVENNIE - EDITOR

Superman CREATED BY Jerry Siegel & Joe Shuster

139

GET REAL, SUGAR-PLUM! OUR DIMENSIONS ONLY CONVERGE EVERY THREE MONTHS. IF I DON'T STRIKE NOW, IT'S GONNA BE *ANOTHER* NINETY DAYS BEFORE I CAN TAKE A POP AT THAT BIG, BLUE DOPE.

THIS WOULDN'T BE THE SAME DOPE WHO OUTSMARTS YOU EVERY TIME YOU SHOW YOUR FACE IN THE THIRD DIMENSION, *Mr.* MXYZPTLK?

SNEAKY DON'T MAKE HIM *SMART, MISS* GSPTLNZ.

FIVE-DIMENSIONAL IMPS GET A FREE PASS IN THE *FOURTH* DIMENSION, RIGHT? I CAN JUMP BACK IN TIME AND PICK A FIGHT WITH THE BLUE BOY BEFORE WE EVEN *MET!*

BESIDES, HE'S *READY* FOR ME NOW WHEN I SLUM IT IN 3-D. THE ELEMENT OF SURPRISE AIN'T ON MY SIDE SINCE HE STARTED MARKIN' OFF MY ARRIVAL DATES ON HIS CALENDAR. *HEY,* WAIT A SEC! WHAT HAVE I BEEN *THINKIN'*?

OUTWITTING AN INEXPERIENCED TEEN OF STEEL SHOULD BE A BREEZE FOR A GUY WITH MY BIG BRAINS! IT'S THE PERFECT ANTI-SUPERMAN PLAN!

BRIGHT IDEAS

HERE WE GO AGAIN...

NOW ALL I HAVE TO DO IS PICK A DAY WHEN POOR SUPES WAS AT HIS MOST VULNERABLE...

SMALLVILLE, U.S.A. THIRTEEN YEARS AGO:

CLARK?

CLARK KENT, WHAT'S SO FASCINATING ABOUT A DAMP SPOT ON THE WALL?

Hm?

SORRY. I WAS IN A WORLD OF MY OWN.

YOU'RE GOING TO HAVE TO WORK ON THAT CONCENTRATION IF YOU WANT TO BE A JOURNALIST WHEN YOU GRADUATE, YOUNG MAN.

CONGRATULATIONS. YOUR CAREER PAPER CAME TOP OF THE CLASS.

I CAN ONLY HOPE YOUR FASHION SKILLS ARE BETTER THAN YOUR SPELLING, MISS LANG. ANOTHER "F" FOR YOUR COLLECTION.

THAT'S BETTER THAN A "G," RIGHT?

THEY DON'T DO "G"S, LANA.

LOOK! UP IN THE SKY!

IT'S A BIRD! IT'S A PLANE...

NO, IT'S CLARK KENT'S BOOKS, LEARNING TO FLY!

HEY!

HaHaHa!

DON'T PUSH ME, BRAD. I'M WARNING YOU.

OH, YEAH? WHAT ARE YOU GONNA DO, KENT? IMPRESS ME TO DEATH WITH YOUR FAMOUS SPELLING ABILITIES?

C'MON, YOU TOLD ME TO BACK OFF AND I LAUGHED IN YOUR FACE. NOW TEACH ME A LESSON THEY DON'T TEACH IN SCHOOL. HIT ME!

DON'T BE SUCH A MORON.

YOUR BEST SHOT ON THE CHIN, CLARKIE-BOY.

IT'S ABOUT TIME I HAD SOME SENSE KNOCKED INTO ME.

HOLY COW!

THWOKK!

WELL, YOU GONNA TAKE THAT SWING OR NOT?

CHICKEN!

YOU CAN BE A REAL LUNKHEAD SOMETIMES, BRAD.

WHAT DO YOU MEAN "SOMETIMES"?

HEY...

"...WHERE'D KENT TAKE OFF IN SUCH A HURRY?"

HI THERE, SKIP. HOW YOU DOIN', BOY?

YOU LOOK LIKE YOU GOT THE WEIGHT OF THE WORLD ON YOUR SHOULDERS, SON. WANT TO SHARE SOME OF THOSE WORRY LINES WITH YOUR OLD MAN?

I'M TIRED OF KEEPING MY POWERS A SECRET, PA. WHY CAN'T I SHOW EVERY-ONE WHAT I CAN DO AND STOP PRETENDING ALL THE TIME?

BECAUSE GOING PUBLIC WILL CHANGE YOUR LIFE FOREVER, CLARK. ONCE PEOPLE KNOW THE TRUTH, THERE'LL BE NO TURNING BACK.

YOU'LL BE HOUNDED WHEREVER YOU GO.

BUT THEY'LL HAVE TO FIND OUT ABOUT ME SOONER OR LATER.

I'VE GOT SO MANY IDEAS HOW TO MAKE THE WORLD A BETTER PLACE.

THESE GIFTS OF MINE COULD CHANGE THINGS FOR EVERYONE.

THE ENTHUSIASM OF YOUTH MUST BE TEMPERED BY THE WISDOM OF EXPERIENCE IF YOU REALLY WANT TO MAKE A DIFFERENCE, SON.

A BOY'S GOT TO LEARN TO BE A *MAN* BEFORE HE KNOWS WHAT IT MEANS TO BE A SUPERMAN.

HE JUST DON'T *GET* IT, *DOES* HE, CLARKIE-BOY?

WHAT THE HECK...?

YOUR POPS MIGHT BE A REGULAR *EINSTEIN* WHEN IT COMES TO MILKIN' CHICKENS, BUT FARMERS AIN'T EXACTLY QUALIFIED TO GIVE ADVICE TO STOWAWAYS FROM THE PLANET KRYPTON!

YOU *KNOW* ABOUT KRYPTON?

SURE. BIG GREEN PLANET. ORBITED A RED SUN 'TIL THE WHOLE PLACE WENT KABLOOEY. YOU'VE HEARD THE STORY, RIGHT?

MY PARENTS TOLD ME THE TRUTH A FEW WEEKS AGO. I WAS SCARED AT FIRST, ANGRY THEY'D LIED TO ME, BUT NOW I REALIZE WHAT A GREAT OPPORTUNITY THIS COULD BE, IF ONLY THEY'D *TRUST* ME.

IS *THIS* WHAT YOU HAD IN MIND?

146

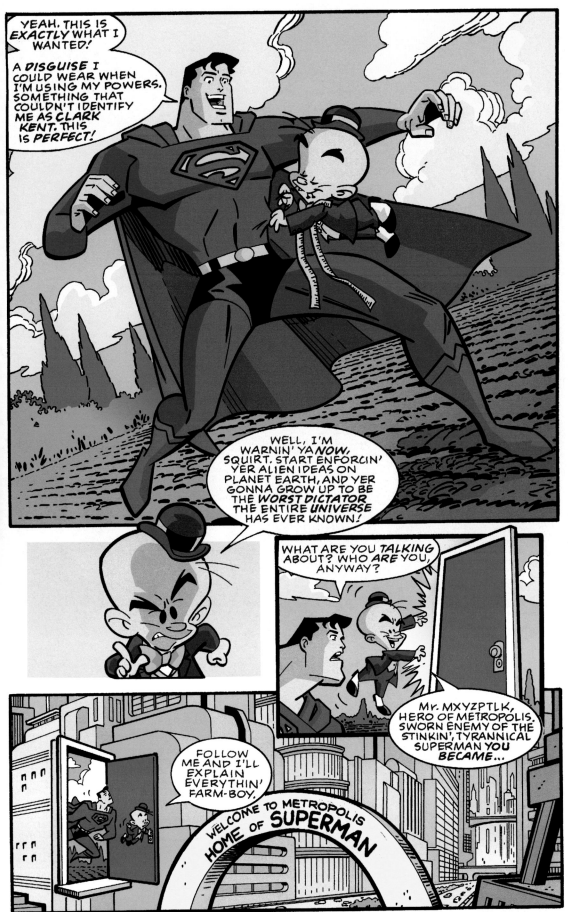

YEAH. THIS IS *EXACTLY* WHAT I WANTED.'

A *DISGUISE* I COULD WEAR WHEN I'M USING MY POWERS. SOMETHING THAT COULDN'T IDENTIFY ME AS *CLARK KENT.* THIS IS *PERFECT!*

WELL, I'M WARNIN' YA *NOW,* SQUIRT. START ENFORCIN' YER ALIEN IDEAS ON PLANET EARTH, AND YER GONNA GROW UP TO BE THE *WORST DICTATOR* THE ENTIRE *UNIVERSE* HAS EVER KNOWN!

WHAT ARE YOU *TALKING* ABOUT? WHO *ARE* YOU, ANYWAY?

MR. MXYZPTLK, HERO OF METROPOLIS. SWORN ENEMY OF THE STINKIN', TYRANNICAL SUPERMAN *YOU BECAME...*

FOLLOW ME AND I'LL EXPLAIN EVERYTHIN' FARM-BOY.

WELCOME TO METROPOLIS HOME OF **SUPERMAN**

147

YA STARTED OUT IN *METROPOLIS* WITH THE BEST OF INTENTIONS, CLOBBERIN' CROOKS AND RESCUIN' KITTENS, BUT TRUTH, JUSTICE AN' THE AMERICAN WAY DIDN'T GIVE YA THE HOTS FOR *LONG*.

AFTER A WHILE, YOU FIGURED *YOU* COULD RUN THE SHOW BETTER THAN THE HALF-WIT *CHIMPANZEES* WHO WERE CALLIN' THE SHOTS DOWN THERE. AN' YOU COULDN'T WAIT TO *SAY* SO, EITHER.

OF COURSE, YOU WEREN'T WITHOUT YOUR *OPPOSITION...*

HEROES LIKE LEX LUTHOR, METALLO, DARKSEID AND THE PARASITE FOUGHT UNDER MY COMMAND IN THE JUSTICE LEAGUE, BUT EVEN *WE* COULDN'T THWART YOUR GLOBAL ASPIRATIONS.

DISSIDENTS WERE SENTENCED TO AN ETERNITY IN THE PHANTOM ZONE, A KRYPTONIAN PRISON MORE PAINFUL THAN ANY EXECUTION. ONLY YOURS TRULY MANAGED TO ESCAPE.

DAILY PLANE

148

THE EMBARRASSING **CLARK KENT** ACT WAS DROPPED LIKE A ROCK AND YOU DID WHAT ANY OTHER SUPER-BEING WOULD DO ON A PLANET FULL OF LAME-BRAINS ALWAYS MAKIN' MISTAKES...

...YOU TOOK OVER THE WORLD.

THE REST OF THE WORLD WAS FORCED TO LIVE IN THE TOTALITARIAN NIGHTMARE YOUR ADOPTIVE PARENTS HAD FEARED SINCE THEY FOUND A CERTAIN ROCKET LYING IN A CERTAIN DITCH...

...LANA LANG MARRIED A MONSTER SHE COULD NEVER LOVE...

...AND SUPERMAN DOMINATED A *TERRIFIED PLANET,* SURROUNDED BY THE SPOILS OF A THOUSAND BATTLES.

YOU STARTIN' TO SEE WHY PA KENT CRIES HIMSELF TO SLEEP EVERY NIGHT AND WISHES HE HAD A NORMAL KID WHO LIKED FOOTBALL?

I'LL *NEVER* BE LIKE... LIKE *THAT!* YOU'VE GOT TO BELIEVE ME!

OH, *SURE,* THAT'S WHAT YOU SAY *NOW,* BUT WE *BOTH* KNOW HOW MUCH YOU WANNA SHOW OFF THOSE FANCY SUPER-POWERS!

THERE'S ONLY *ONE* WAY TO MAKE SURE YOU NEVER HURT THE PEOPLE YOU LOVE...

...AND THAT'S TO *EXILE* YOURSELF FROM EARTH.

I CAME BACK IN TIME TO *BEG* YOU TO *LEAVE*, TO REACH ANY SHRED OF *HUMANITY* YOU MIGHT HAVE *HAD*, BUT THE FINAL DECISION IS *YOURS*, DOES EARTH HAVE A CHANCE TO PROSPER ON ITS OWN, OR IS IT A FUTURE OF *SUPER-SLAVERY?*

IS...IS THERE ANYWHERE I CAN GO WHERE PEOPLE WILL BE *SAFE?*

THAT'S A QUESTION I'VE THOUGHT LONG AND HARD ABOUT, SON, AND AFTER *MUCH* DELIBERATION, I'VE FINALLY COME TO A DECISION...

BANG! *ZOOM!!* STRAIGHT TO DA MOON!

CAN YOUR MAGIC FIX IT FOR ME TO BREATHE UP THERE?

PIECE OF CAKE! WHEN DO YOU WANNA BOOK YOUR SEAT ON THE *FIVE-DIMENSIONAL EXPRESS*, SUPER-BRAT? JUST SAY THE WORD!

LET'S GO BEFORE MA AND PA WAKE UP. IT'S PROBABLY EASIER FOR *EVERYONE* IF I DON'T SAY GOODBYE IN PERSON.

LAND *SAKES*, JONATHAN. STOP STEALING THE *COVERS*.

Mm?

MAYBE MAN WILL FIND A WAY TO LIVE ON THE MOON, AND I'LL GET TO TALK TO SOMEONE AGAIN SOMEDAY, *huh?*

HECK, I DON'T SEE WHY BEING BANNED FROM EARTH SHOULD MEAN YOU CAN'T HAVE A *LITTLE* COMPANIONSHIP, KID...

SKIP!

NAH! "SKIP" WAS THE NAME *CLARK KENT* GAVE HIS MUTT.

YOU SHOULD GO FOR A SENTIMENTAL TRIBUTE TO YOUR HOME-WORLD AS A POIGNANT REMINDER OF EVERYTHIN' YOU'VE *LOST*.

ARF! ARF!

"*EARTHO*" KINDA HAS A RING TO IT.

YOU WON'T FORGET ABOUT ME, WILL YOU, Mr. MXYZPTLK?

KIDDO, SUPERBOY IS GONNA BE HAILED AS THE GREATEST *HERO* WHO EVER *LIVED* WHEN I GET MY BUTT BACK TO THE FUTURE.

YOU'VE SAVED THE WORLD PLEDGIN' TO DO NOTHIN'. I *SALUTE* YOU, BABY. YOUR *COUNTRY* SALUTES YOU. THE ENTIRE *PLANET* OWES YOU BIG-TIME!

WELL, GOTTA GO. SEE YA!

POOF!

153

BACK IN THE PRESENT...

I DON'T BELIEVE IT! I FINALLY OUTWITTED SUPER-HAM!

LITTLE CLARKIE QUITTIN' BEFORE HE EVEN *STARTS* HIS CAREER MEANS METROPOLIS IS NOW A *SUPERMAN-FREE ZONE!*

MXY, BABY, YOU JUST WIPED THE LAST SON OF KREEPTON FROM THE HISTORY BOOKS! IT'S *CELEBRATION TIME!*

HOLD ONTO YOUR HATS, YOU FUNNY LITTLE DOTS...

METROPO

MONORAIL S

REALITY'S ABOUT TO GET A *FIVE-DIMENSIONAL FACE LIFT!*

AIN'T METROPOLIS A *SCREAM* WHEN THAT BIG, BLUE CHUMP AIN'T AROUND TO SPOIL EVERYONE'S FUN?

TOYS 4 U

THE TOYS-- THEY'VE COME ALIVE!

TCHAK! TCHAK! TCHAK!

SUPES WOULD NORMALLY APPEAR NOW AND TRY TO GET RID OF ME USING ONE OF HIS LOUSY TRICKS, BUT THE BAD OLD DAYS ARE GONE FOREVER, BOYS AND GIRLS...

...GET READY FOR THE WHITE-KNUCKLE RIDE OF YOUR LIVES!

PERRY WHITE ACTING OUT KING KONG'S LAST STAND... METROPOLIS BRIDGE TURNING INTO SPAGHETTI... AND WE'VE GOT A JELLO-BASED VEHICLE COLLISION ON A STRAWBERRY ICE CREAM HIGHWAY, CAPTAIN SAWYER!

ANY CHANCE OF ASSISTANCE?

NOT UNTIL WE WRAP UP THE TOAD STOOL RIOTS, UNIT SEVEN.

OUTTA THE WAY, ROAD-HOG!

C'MON, YA WIMPS! PUT UP YOUR DUKES AN' FIGHT!

DON'T TELL ME SUPES WAS THE ONLY GUY IN TOWN WITH THE GUTS TO GO A FEW ROUNDS WITH A FIFTH-DIMEN-SIONAL IMP!

TO MXYZOP

MR. MXYZPTLK

GEEZ! IT LOOKS LIKE EARTH MINUS THE BEEFCAKE'S REALLY GONE DOWNHILL!

LEX LUTHOR, THE MOST POWERFUL MAN ALIVE...

LOIS LANE, DEAD IN A CHOPPER CRASH...

THE OLSEN BRAT, CRIPPLED IN AN INTER-GANG ATTACK...

LOIS LANE

MA AND PA KENT, DYIN' OF BROKEN HEARTS, 'COS THEIR BLUE-EYED BOY DISAPPEARED ONE NIGHT AND NEVER CAME HOME.

THIS WOULD BRING TEARS TO A GLASS EYE!

FOR SALE

AS MUCH AS I HATE TO ADMIT IT, SUPES WAS PROBABLY THE ONLY THING THAT MADE THE THIRD DIMENSION TOLERABLE!

MAYBE GETTIN' RID OF THE OLD HUNK IN TRUNKS WASN'T SUCH A SMART IDEA, AFTER ALL.

POOF!

156

BACK IN THE PAST...

C'MON, BLUE BOY. YOU AN' ME ARE GOIN' BACK TO SMALLVILLE AND HAVE OURSELVES A FEW LAUGHS.

POOF!

?

Huh? BUT YOU SAID EARTH WAS DOOMED IF I DIDN'T STAY ON THE MOON!

I WUZ LYIN', BONEHEAD! DO I LOOK LIKE A METROPOLIS MARVEL?

I'M AN IMP FROM ANOTHER DIMENSION WHO WANTED SUPERMAN ERASED FROM THE FUTURE, BUT NOW I GOT A NEW PLAN!

BAD GUY

Y'SEE, ME AN' YOUR ADULT SELF LOCK HORNS EVERY 90 DAYS, BUT WE'VE GOT AN ARRANGEMENT WHERE I DISAPPEAR IF HE MAKES ME SAY MY NAME BACKWARDS TWICE.

I'M OFFERIN' YOU THE SAME DEAL!

BATTLE of the CENTURY EVERY 90 DAYS!

SUPERMAN vs MXYZPTLK

BUT I GOTTA WARN YA, KID--I KNOW EVERY TRICK YOU'RE GONNA PULL, AN' COUNTLESS DEFEATS MEAN I AIN'T GONNA FALL FOR ANY OF 'EM!

GET READY FOR BATTLE-GROUND SMALLVILLE, "SUPERBOY!"

SNIF SNIF

NOT A CHANCE, MISTER

FORGET IT.

I LIED WHEN I SAID YOU WERE GONNA GROW UP TO BE A DICTATOR, SUPER-DOPE! HOW MANY TIMES BEFORE IT SINKS IN?!

THAT'S NOT WHAT I'M TALKING ABOUT.

IT'S JUST THAT I DON'T WANT TO PLAY YOUR STUPID GAME FOR THE REST OF MY LIFE, MXYZPTLK. IT SOUNDS REALLY BORING.

"BORING"? WHADDAYA MEAN, "BORING"?

DUMB. JUVENILE. STRICTLY FOR KIDS.

I'M SIXTEEN YEARS OLD. I'M NOT GOING TO TRY TO TRICK SOMEONE INTO SAYING HIS NAME BACKWARDS. THAT'S PATHETIC.

"PATHETIC"? "PATHETIC"?!

GET YOUR BUTT BACK DOWN TO EARTH AND PLAY MY GAME!

Uh-uh.

PLEASE! PLEASE! PLEASE! PLEASE! PLEASE!

NOT IN A MILLION YEARS.

PEDESTALS R-US
WHEN YOU GOTTA STAND FOR SOMETHING

Y'KNOW SOMETHING, KID? YOU'RE AN EVEN BIGGER PAIN IN THE NECK THAN YOUR STINKIN' ADULT SELF!

KLTPZYXM! KLTPZYXM!

POOF!

158

I'D RATHER SPEND THE NEXT NINETY DAYS IN THE FIFTH DIMENSION THAN WASTE 'EM ARGUING HERE WITH YOU, PEA-BRAIN!

I STILL WON'T PLAY WHEN YOU COME BACK.

BUSTER, I'M NEVER COMING BACK, AND I'LL MAKE SURE YOU WON'T EVEN REMEMBER THIS! SEE YOU AROUND, KIDDO!

A LOTTA LAUGHS THIS WASN'T!

POOF!

Huh?

WOW! WHAT ARE WE DOING OUT HERE SO EARLY, SKIP?

GUESS I MUST HAVE BEEN SLEEP-WALKING, huh?

?

WELL, C'MON, BOY-- LET'S GET SOME BREAKFAST AND PLAY WITH YOUR BALL BEFORE I TAKE OFF FOR SCHOOL.

159

MORE PANCAKES AND MAPLE SYRUP, ANYONE?

GIVE 'EM TO CLARK, MARTHA. HE'S GOING TO NEED PLENTY OF BUILDING UP IF HE'S *SERIOUS* ABOUT THIS SUPERHERO CAREER.

ACTUALLY, I THINK I MIGHT WAIT A WHILE, PA...

I FIGURE THE WORLD'LL FEEL A LOT BETTER ABOUT A SUPER*MAN* WHO KNOWS WHAT HE'S DOING, AS OPPOSED TO A SUPER*BOY* WHO'S JUST LEARNING THE ROPES, RIGHT?

THAT'S A VERY *WISE* DECISION, SON.

BY THE WAY, I HAD A DREAM LAST NIGHT THAT MIGHT SOLVE THE *PRIVACY* PROBLEM WHEN YOU DECIDE TO GO PUBLIC. A COSTUME IDEA FOR A KIND OF *SECRET* IDENTITY...

LET'S SEE, JONATHAN.

IT'S KINDA *ROUGH* IN PLACES, BUT I GET THE FEELING I'M REALLY ON TO SOMETHING *GOOD* HERE.

The End

160

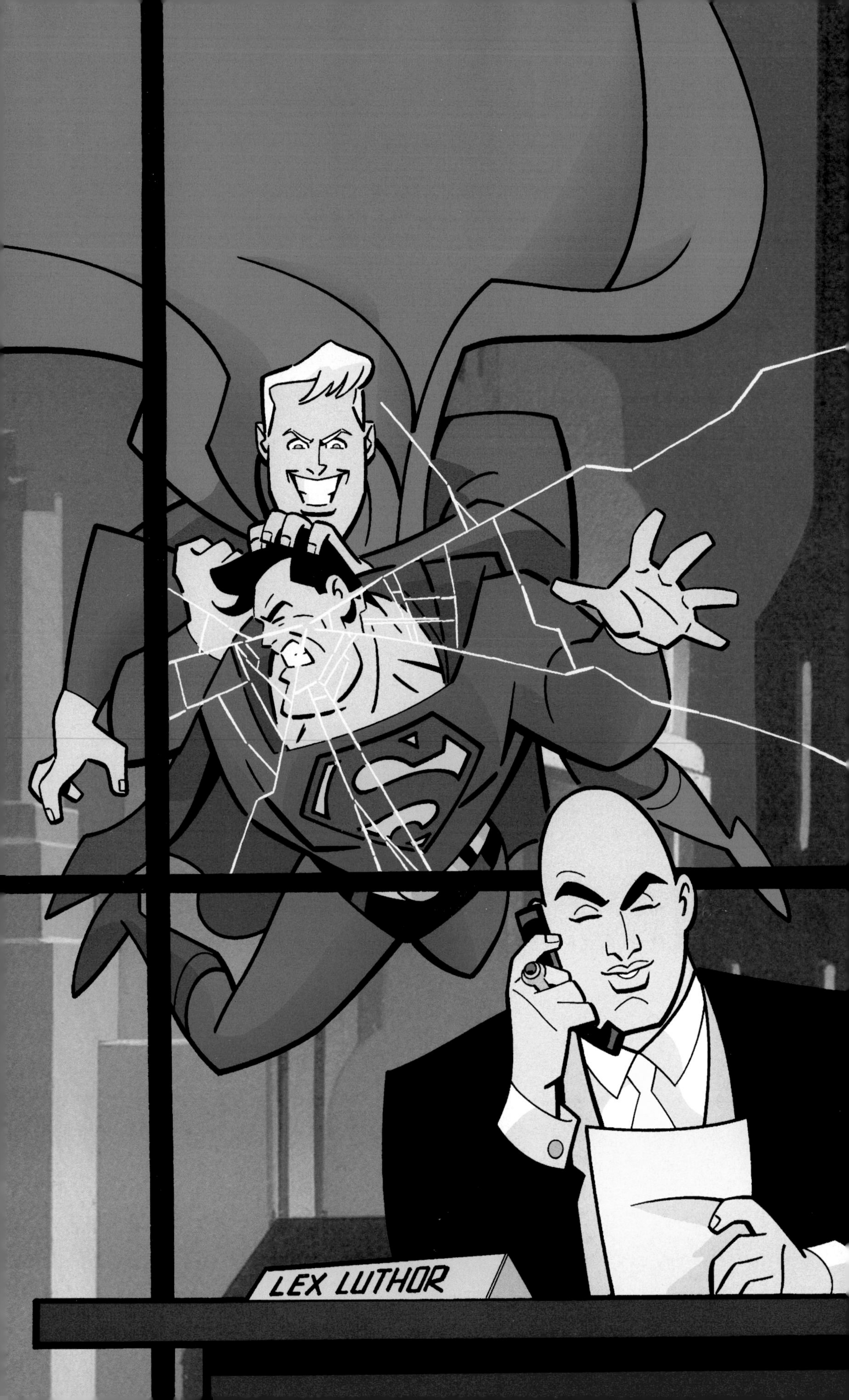
LEX LUTHOR

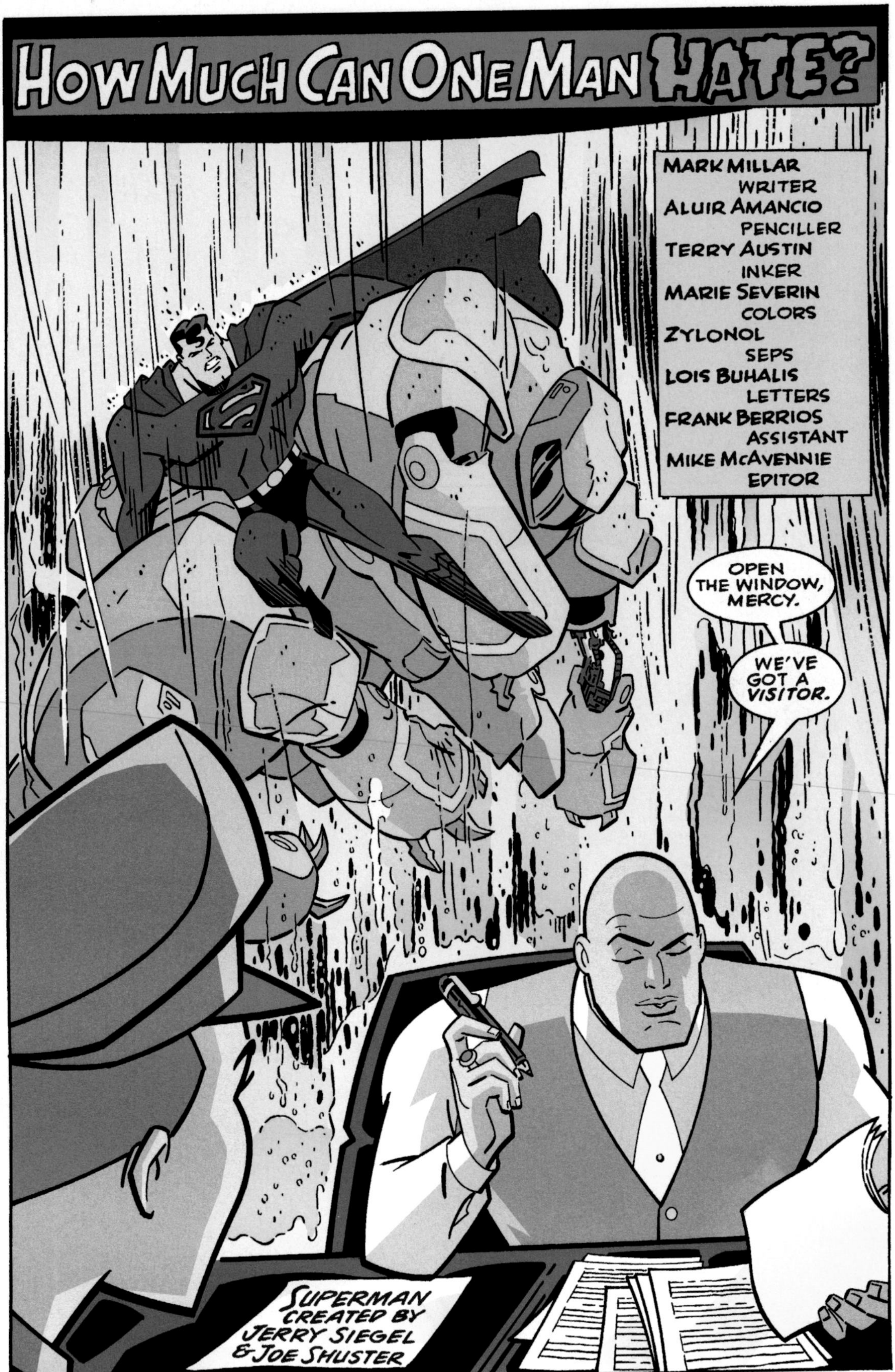
HOW MUCH CAN ONE MAN HATE?
MARK MILLAR WRITER
ALUIR AMANCIO PENCILLER
TERRY AUSTIN INKER
MARIE SEVERIN COLORS
ZYLONOL SEPS
LOIS BUHALIS LETTERS
FRANK BERRIOS ASSISTANT
MIKE McAVENNIE EDITOR
OPEN THE WINDOW, MERCY.
WE'VE GOT A VISITOR.
SUPERMAN CREATED BY JERRY SIEGEL & JOE SHUSTER

VRRRRRRRR

KILLER ANDROIDS PROGRAMMED TO TRACK DOWN MY DENSE MOLECULAR STRUCTURE? A LITTLE UNINSPIRED BY EVEN *YOUR* STANDARDS, LUTHOR.

CLIK!

AS USUAL, SUPERMAN, YOU HAVE ME *COMPLETELY* AT A LOSS.

WHUDD!

STOP PLAYING GAMES, LEX. A LITTLE X-RAY INSPECTION CONFIRMS EVERY NUT AND BOLT IN THESE THINGS CAME FROM THIS BUILDING.

YOU MIGHT AS WELL HAVE LEFT YOUR *WALLET* AND *DRIVER'S LICENSE* AT THE SCENE OF THE CRIME.

BELIEVE ME, SUPERMAN, EVEN *YOU* WITH YOUR GREAT STRENGTH WOULD HAVE TROUBLE LIFTING MY WALLET.

AND AS FOR THOSE BITS AND PIECES USED TO BUILD YOUR LITTLE PLAY-MATES...

...YOU'LL FIND THEY WERE STOLEN FROM OUR WAREHOUSE BY A CRAZED EX-EMPLOYEE WITH A GRUDGE AGAINST A CERTAIN MAN OF STEEL.

CHECK THE FILES FOR YOURSELF IF YOU DON'T BELIEVE ME.

OH, I'M SURE THEY'RE ALL IN *PERFECT* ORDER.

WHAT'S THE MATTER, SUPERMAN? YOU'RE STARTING TO SOUND A LITTLE *PARANOID.* DON'T TELL ME THE JOB'S STARTING TO GET TO YOU.

STILL, THE NUMBER OF PSYCHOPATHS OUT THERE TRYING TO KILL YOU ON A DAILY BASIS *MUST* BE RATHER STRESSFUL. AFTER ALL, *THEY* ONLY HAVE TO BE LUCKY *ONCE,* BUT *YOU* HAVE TO BE LUCKY *ALL* THE TIME.

WHY DO YOU *DO* IT, LUTHOR? WHY DO YOU WASTE ALL THIS TIME AND ENERGY? IS IT THE POWERS? IS IT THAT I HAVE HAIR?

WHAT HAVE I EVER DONE TO MAKE YOU HATE ME THIS MUCH?

IF YOU HAVE TO ASK, YOU'LL NEVER KNOW.

MANIAC.

LEXCORP

165

HOW MUCH DID HE COST ME TODAY, MERCY?

ONLY TEN MILLION BUCKS, BOSS. A FEW HUNDRED LESS THAN THE ROBOT DUPLICATE YOU DESIGNED A FEW MONTHS AGO...

...AND A FRACTION OF THE PRICE YOU PAID FOR THE BIZARRO PROGRAM, THE GALACTIC GOLEM OR THE HAMMER OF HATE.

WE'RE ALMOST ON BUDGET FOR A CHANGE THIS MONTH.

THAT DOESN'T EXCUSE THE FACT THAT A CREATURE OF NO OBVIOUS INTELLIGENCE HAS THWARTED ME YET AGAIN, MERCY...

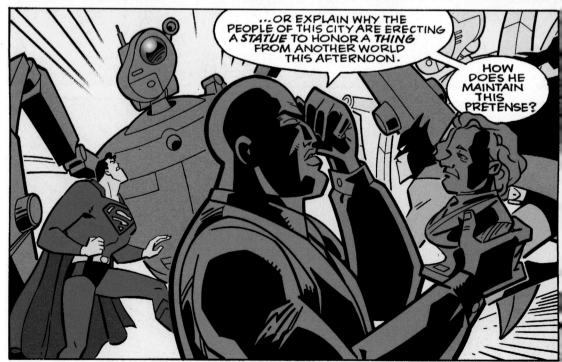

...OR EXPLAIN WHY THE PEOPLE OF THIS CITY ARE ERECTING A STATUE TO HONOR A THING FROM ANOTHER WORLD THIS AFTERNOON.

HOW DOES HE MAINTAIN THIS PRETENSE?

WHO WILL RID ME OF THIS TERRIBLE BEING?!

SHKREESH!

CLEANERS, VIDEO REPAIR AND A NEW BUST OF EINSTEIN FOR THE DESK.

FETCH THE CAR, MERCY. WE'VE GOT AN APPOINTMENT TO KEEP IN CENTENNIAL PARK.

ARE YOU SURE WATCHING THE MAYOR UNVEIL A STATUE OF SUPERMAN IS A SMART IDEA WHEN YOU'RE IN THIS KINDA MOOD, BOSS?

SMART IDEAS ARE HOW I STAY IN BUSINESS, MERCY...

"...BESIDES, WHAT GREATER SOURCE OF INSPIRATION FOR A NEW PLAN THAN WATCHING THEM LINE UP TO TOUCH THE HEM OF HIS CAPE?"

IT'S GETTING LATE, BOSS. EVERYONE ELSE LEFT HOURS AGO.

IS THIS STATUE REALLY SUCH A BIG DEAL? I MEAN, HOW MANY SCHOOLS AND HOSPITALS HAVE YOUR NAME ABOVE THE DOORWAY, *huh*?

ALL PAID FOR WITH MY OWN MONEY, MERCY.

THIS NEVER COST SUPERMAN A PENNY.

NEW PLAN BEGINNING TO FORM?

STUDY MY EXPRESSION AND DECIDE FOR YOURSELF, MY DEAR.

THIS IS OUR MOST PERFECT SCHEME YET.

I STILL CAN'T BELIEVE HE STOOD EVERYONE UP, Mr. KENT.

WELL, HE'S NEVER BEEN THE TYPE TO STICK AROUND AND WAIT TO BE THANKED, JIMMY. I GUESS SUPERMAN JUST FINDS THIS KIND OF PUBLIC ATTENTION A LITTLE... UNCOMFORTABLE.

DAILY PLAN

SUPERMAN DECLIN STATUE INVITATION

WHY WOULD SUPERMAN DISAPPOINT PEOPLE LIKE THAT?

AND WHEN DID YOU BECOME SUCH AN AUTHORITY, SMALLVILLE?

OLSEN!

WHAT ARE YOU DOING SITTING AROUND STARING INTO YOUR COFFEE BEANS WHEN TOMORROW'S FRONT PAGE IS UNFOLDING DOWNTOWN?

ORDINARY CREEP OR SUPER-CREEP, CHIEF?

DEFINITELY THE LATTER, LOIS. THE PARASITE'S CRAWLED OUT FROM WHATEVER ROCK HE WAS HIDING UNDER.

SAY, WHERE'D KENT GO?

169

GUESS THE PARASITE SURVIVED OUR LAST ENCOUNTER AFTER ALL, CAPTAIN.

ONE THING I'VE LEARNED IN THIS JOB IS THAT THE BAD GUYS *NEVER* STAY DEAD FOR LONG, SUPERMAN. WE'VE GOT HIM CORNERED DOWNSTAIRS IN THE SUBWAY STATION.

WHUMM?!

APPARENTLY NOT FOR MUCH LONGER.

BETTER KEEP YOUR BOYS BACK, MAGGIE. THIS IS GOING TO GET PRETTY ROUGH.

Um, SUPERMAN, THE PARASITE DIDN'T THROW THAT PUNCH...

...HE WAS ON THE *RECEIVING* END!

Huh?!

TAKE ALL THE PICTURES YOU WANT, BOYS AND GIRLS. JUST BE SURE TO CATCH MY BEST SIDE FOR THE LADIES.

NICE JOB, FRIEND. IT'S ALWAYS A PLEASURE TO MEET SOMEONE ELSE IN THE SAME LINE OF WORK. WHAT DO YOU CALL YOURSELF?

SUPERIOR-MAN, OF COURSE! HOW ELSE DO YOU DESCRIBE THE ONE GUY IN METROPOLIS STRONGER THAN SUPERMAN?

GET USED TO THE NAME, FOLKS. IT'S GOING TO BE EVERYWHERE ONCE I CATCH THE CROOKS THE MAN OF STEEL COULDN'T.

LOIS LANE, DAILY PLANET. ARE YOU SAYING SUPERMAN HAS A PARTNER?

OH, NOT A PARTNER, GORGEOUS...

...A REPLACEMENT.

171

AFTER CAPTURING A VILLAIN SUPERMAN ALLOWED TO SLIP THROUGH HIS FINGERS, SUPERIOR-MAN HAS SINCE WOWED METROPOLIS BY SAVING THE CITY FROM THE MONSTROUS KALIBAK...

...ARRESTING THE EVER-ELUSIVE TOYMAN...

...SUBDUING TITANO, THE SUPER-APE, RECENTLY FREED FROM HIS ISLAND SANCTUARY BY ANIMAL RIGHTS ACTIVISTS...

...AND BRINGING ALMOST EVERY WANTED GOON IN METROPOLIS TO JUSTICE, DECLARING THE CITY A VIRTUAL CRIME-FREE ZONE.

IS IT ANY WONDER PEOPLE ARE SUDDENLY ASKING IF WE STILL NEED A SUPERMAN?

172

BUT MOST DRAMATIC OF ALL IS THE STATEMENT ABOUT TO BE MADE HERE AT THE HEADQUARTERS OF LEXCORP INTERNATIONAL...

LADIES AND GENTLEMEN, LEXCORP IS PROUD TO ANNOUNCE OUR FORMAL PARTNERSHIP WITH SUPERIOR-MAN IN LIGHT OF THE BREATHTAKING CHANGES HE'S MADE TO METROPOLIS IN SUCH A SHORT TIME.

KLIK KLIK! FAASH!

COMBINING OUR TECHNOLOGY WITH HIS STRENGTH AND ENTHUSIASM, WE FIRMLY BELIEVE WE CAN TURN THIS CITY INTO A UTOPIA.

THE SKY IS NO LONGER THE LIMIT.

FAASH!

KLIK KLIK

THE NEW HERO'S FANS IN METROPOLIS WERE ECSTATIC.

A PLAIN-SPEAKING ATTITUDE THAT APPEALS TO EVERYONE.

TACKLING PROBLEMS EVEN SUPERMAN DIDN'T TOUCH.

BUT ONE QUESTION STILL REMAINS:

WHO IS SUPERIOR-MAN, AND WHERE DID HE COME FROM?

MISSING

TRACKING DOWN LOST CATS WITH YOUR X-RAY VISION, SUPERMAN? TELL ME IT HASN'T COME TO *THIS*.

WHAT'S *NEXT*, BLUE-BOY? HELPING OLD LADIES CROSS THE STREET? CLEARING SNOW FROM PEOPLE'S DRIVEWAYS?

UNLIKE *YOU*, I DON'T DO THIS FOR THE PUBLICITY, FRIEND.

SO ME GRABBING ALL THOSE HEADLINES *DOESN'T* BOTHER YOU?

BEING RELEGATED TO *NUMBER TWO* ISN'T GOING TO DRIVE YOU OUT OF TOWN LIKE I FIGURED?

DREAM ON, MISTER. I'M HERE TO STAY.

WELL, IN THAT CASE, SUPERMAN, I'VE GOT A MESSAGE TO DELIVER FROM *LEX LUTHOR*...

KA-WHAMMM!

REST IN PEACE, FREAK!

LUTHOR? WHY IS IT --$NNGH$-- ALWAYS LUTHOR?

ARE YOU THE LATEST "ULTIMATE WEAPON" HE'S BUILT TO ASSASSINATE ME?

ACTUALLY, THE IDEA WAS TO REPLACE YOU, SUPERMAN.

SHOW YOU HOW HUMILIATING IT FEELS TO BE THE PEOPLE'S FAVORITE ONE MINUTE, AND OBSOLETE THE NEXT.

ARRGH!

KILLING YOU WAS JUST THE BACKUP PLAN.

THWAK!

THAT WAS KRYPTONITE-VISION, FLY-BOY. JUST ONE OF THE POWERS LUTHOR GAVE ME FOR THE NEW METROPOLIS WE PLAN TO RULE.

HE KNEW BETTER THAN ANY-ONE HOW A FLASHY NEW HERO WAS ALL IT TOOK TO MAKE THEM FORGET ALL THE GOOD WORK YOU'VE DONE.

TURN YOUR BACK FOR A SECOND AND THESE MAGGOTS ARE WORSHIP-ING SOMEONE ELSE.

SOME OF US DON'T DO IT FOR GRATITUDE, BUSTER...

...BUT I GUESS THAT'S SOMETHING YOU'LL NEVER UNDERSTAND.

KRAK

KOOM

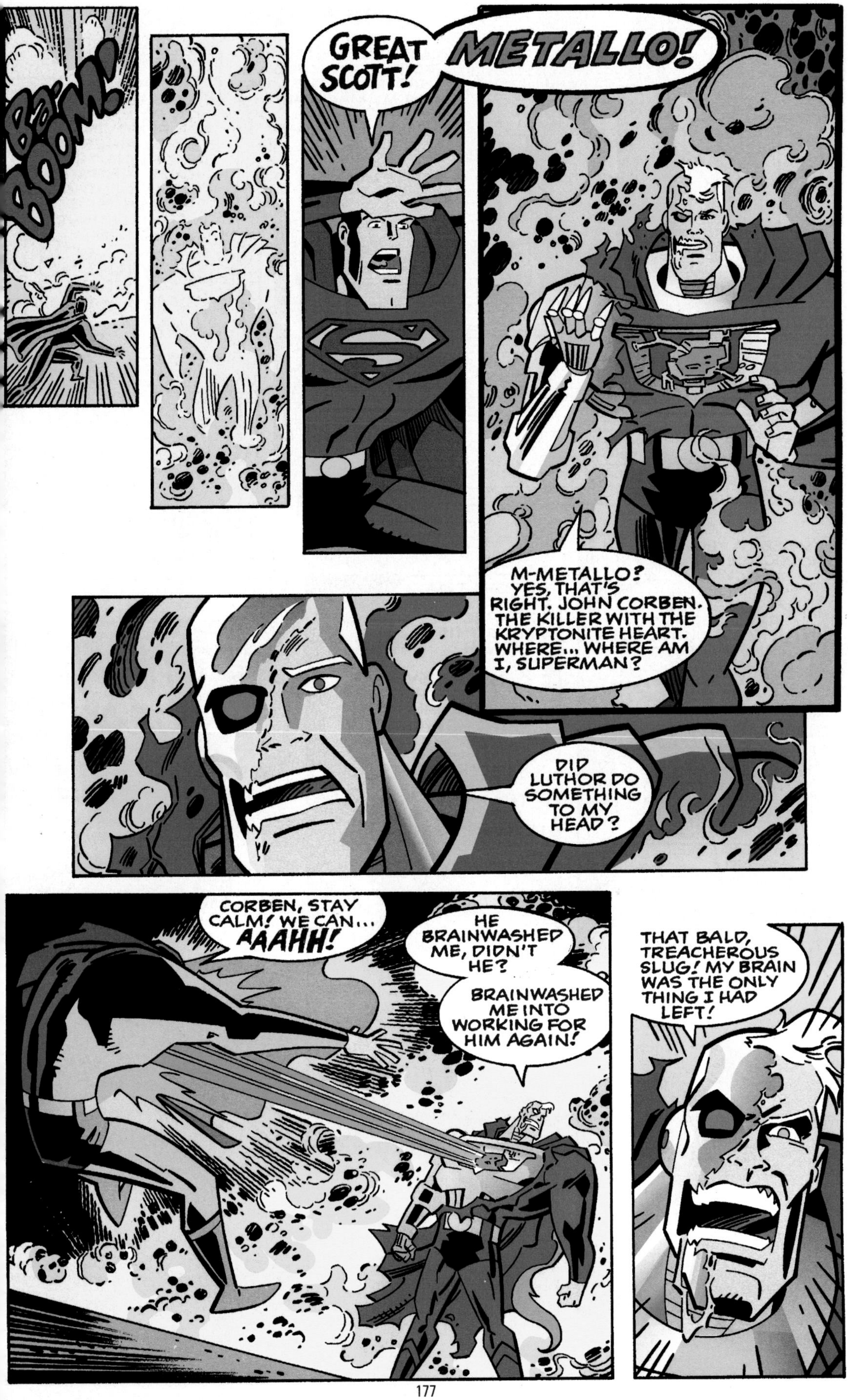
BA-BOOM!
GREAT SCOTT!
METALLO!
M-METALLO? YES, THAT'S RIGHT. JOHN CORBEN. THE KILLER WITH THE KRYPTONITE HEART. WHERE... WHERE AM I, SUPERMAN?
DID LUTHOR DO SOMETHING TO MY HEAD?
CORBEN, STAY CALM! WE CAN... AAAHH!
HE BRAINWASHED ME, DIDN'T HE?
BRAINWASHED ME INTO WORKING FOR HIM AGAIN!
THAT BALD, TREACHEROUS SLUG! MY BRAIN WAS THE ONLY THING I HAD LEFT!

NOTHING NUMBS THE TASTE BUDS LIKE THE FRIVOLOUS CHATTER OF THE *COGS* IN MY *MACHINE*, MY DEAR...

THANK THE MANAGER ON MY BEHALF FOR REMOVING THE NEARBY DINERS AND REFUNDING THEIR MONEY. INFORM HIM THAT LEX LUTHOR IS MOST SATISFIED WITH HIS BUSINESS SENSE.

IT'S BEEN A VERY PRODUCTIVE MONTH, MERCY.

SUPERMAN REPLACED AS THE HERO OF METROPOLIS, HIS SUCCESSOR UNDER MY ABSOLUTE CONTROL, AND A PURPOSE FOR METALLO, AFTER ALL.

YOU CAN TELL OMEGA SECTOR TO EXPECT A BONUS THIS MONTH.

IT ISN'T EVERY DAY OUR PEOPLE REPROGRAM A REVENGE-CHARGED SUPER-VILLAIN, HELL-BENT ON DESTROYING ME.

THAT MUST BE WORTH A FEW LEXCORP NECKTIES, AT LEAST.

KKRUNCH!

BETTER *CANCEL* THAT MEMO, MERCY...

THE "REVENGE-CHARGED SUPER-VILLAIN" IS *BACK* FOR *REVENGE.*

METALLO, *NO!*

DON'T WASTE YOUR *BREATH,* LEX, OLD PAL.

MY BRAINWASHING WAS *REVERSED* WHEN SUPERMAN BURNED OFF THAT SYNTHETIC SKIN YOU COVERED ME WITH...

KRUNCH!

CHANG!

Skrissh!

REENCH!

...NOW I'M FINALLY GOING TO MAKE YOU *PAY* FOR TURNING ME INTO THIS *FRANKENSTEIN'S MONSTER!*

BOSS! LOOK WHAT HE'S DONE TO THE *CHOPPER!*

I'M GOING TO MAKE YOU *EAT* THIS, YOU SLIME-BALL.

VERY *VERY* SLOWLY...

WHOKK!

WHAT THE HECK?

SUPERMAN. DON'T YOU KNOW WHEN YOU'RE BEATEN?

WHAT ARE YOU DOING WEARING THAT RIDICULOUS COSTUME?

SWEET DREAMS, METALLO.

SEE YOU IN THE CELLS WHEN WE RECONNECT YOU LATER.

OH, NO.

LEAD-LINED RADIATION SUIT FROM YOUR FRIENDS AT S.T.A.R. LABS?

CLEVER BOY, LUTHOR. RIGHT THE FIRST TIME.

YOU TWO OKAY?

SLINK

WHY *SHOULDN'T* WE BE?

EVERYTHING WAS UNDER MY ABSOLUTE CONTROL, SUPERMAN.

"ABSOLUTE CONTROL"?

I SAW A MAN SO CONSUMED BY HIS OWN MADNESS THAT HE ALMOST KILLED HIMSELF THIS TIME!

HOW MANY FIENDISH PLOTS AND DEATH-RAYS ARE THERE GOING TO *BE*, LUTHOR? HOW MANY *BILLIONS* OF DOLLARS ARE YOU GOING TO *WASTE*?

YOU WERE BLESSED WITH A *BRILLIANT* MIND. YOU COULD MAKE THE WORLD SUCH A *WONDERFUL* PLACE.

STOP WASTING YOUR LIFE TRYING TO *DESTROY* IT.

181

YOU STILL THINKING ABOUT WHAT SUPERMAN SAID, BOSS?

YES, MERCY, I'VE BEEN GIVING IT RATHER A LOT OF CONSIDERATION.

EXTRA! SUPERIOR-MAN REVEALED AS METALLO

I'VE SPENT EIGHT BILLION DOLLARS TRYING TO DESTROY HIM IN THE LAST FINANCIAL YEAR, AND TEN HOURS EVERY DAY DEVISING DEATH-TRAPS.

WHAT HAVE I ACCOMPLISHED? ABSOLUTELY *NOTHING.*

AND NOW YOU THINK IT'S TIME TO CALL IT *QUITS?* SPEND YOUR MONEY ON SOMETHING *USEFUL?* MAYBE TAKE A LITTLE *VACATION TIME?*

AFTER THAT PATRONIZING LITTLE RANT ABOUT WHAT I SHOULD BE DOING WITH MY LIFE? *ABSOLUTELY NOT!*

NEXT YEAR'S BUDGET WILL INCREASE TO *TWENTY BILLION!* *SIXTEEN* HOURS EVERY DAY MUST BE DEVOTED TO HIS ABSOLUTE *NONEXISTENCE!*

A PLAN IS ALREADY BEGINNING TO FORM, MERCY...

I BELIEVE THIS IS MY MOST PERFECT SCHEME YET.

LEXCORP

YEARS AGO...

WATCHA DOIN' HIDIN' IN YOUR ROOM, LEX? WRITIN' A FANCY ITALIAN OPERA OR SOMETHIN'?

IF YOU REALLY *MUST* KNOW, FATHER, I AM CONSTRUCTING A MODEL OF THE LEXCORP HEADQUARTERS I PLAN TO BUILD IN METROPOLIS THIRTEEN YEARS FROM NOW.

LOOK AT IT-- THE *TALLEST* BUILDING IN ALL THE CITY. *MAGNIFICENT*, ISN'T IT?

LEXCORP

WHERE'D I GO *WRONG* WITH YOU, BOY? WHY CAN'T YA STOP MAKIN' PLANS FOR A CHANGE AND PLAY BALL WITH OTHER KIDS SOMETIMES?

YOU'RE *SEVEN YEARS OLD*, FOR CRIPES' SAKE!

PRECISELY, FATHER. TIME IS MY ALLY, AND I HAVE *NO* INTENTION OF RESIDING IN THIS *WRETCHED* APARTMENT BEYOND THE AGE OF TEN.

THIS IS GOING TO BE THE HEART OF A MULTI-NATIONAL BUSINESS EMPIRE ENVIED FROM ONE END OF THE WORLD TO THE OTHER.

ONE DAY, *LEX LUTHOR* IS GOING TO LOOK DOWN UPON METROPOLIS...

"...AND EVERYONE IS GOING TO LOOK UP TO *ME*."

END

JONATHAN KENT
BELOVED HUSBAND
AND FATHER

MARTHA KENT
BELOVED WIFE
AND MOTHER

MANLEY·ouslin

FAMILY REUNION

PART ONE

MARK MILLAR — WRITER
ALUIR AMANCIO — PENCILLER
TERRY AUSTIN — INKER
MARIE SEVERIN — COLORIST
ZYLONOL — SEPARATOR
PHIL FELIX — LETTERER
FRANK BERRIOS — ASSISTANT
MIKE McAVENNIE — EDITOR

ATTENTION! CLEAR S.T.A.R. LABS OF ALL PERSONNEL!

WARNING! THIS IS NOT A DRILL!

SUPERMAN CREATED BY JERRY SIEGEL & JOE SHUSTER

187

EVACUATING THE PLACE IS *POINTLESS*, PROFESSOR! THIS ANTIMATTER ENGINE'S GONNA BITE A HOLE IN THE *WORLD* WHEN IT BLOWS!

THEN WE CAN EITHER GIVE UP AND *DIE*, OR TRY TO *REPAIR* THIS THING! WHICH- EVER YOU PREFER, THERE'S ONLY A MINUTE LEFT!

BOOOM!

WOW! WHAT THE HECK WAS *THAT*?

DO YOU REALLY NEED TO *ASK*?

"THE CHIPS WERE DOWN...

"...ALL HOPE WAS LOST...

"...WHO ELSE COULD IT POSSIBLY *BE*?"

188

MOST EXPENSIVE FIREWORKS DISPLAY WE'LL EVER SEE, HUH?

EIGHTEEN MONTHS AND TEN MILLION DOLLARS' WORTH OF RESEARCH IS *SMALL CHANGE* NEXT TO FIVE BILLION LIVES, MY DEAR.

THIS JUST PROVES OUR ANTI-MATTER ENGINE WASN'T *QUITE* THE SAFE, CLEAN SOURCE OF ALTERNATIVE ENERGY WE *HOPED* IT MIGHT BE.

PROFESSOR? WHAT'S *WRONG?*

FORTUNATELY FOR *US*, SUPERMAN WAS AROUND TO ...

GOOD LORD ...!

NO TIME TO CONSOLE PROFESSOR HAMILTON. MY INTERGANG CONTACT SAID HE'D CALL SHORTLY AFTER LUNCH...

...WHICH MEANS THERE'S NO TIME TO GRAB FOOD AT THE PRESS CLUB, EITHER.

A HOT DOG, PLEASE, TONY. HEAVY ON THE MUSTARD.

COMIN' RIGHT UP...

SAY, DON'T I KNOW YOU FROM SOME-PLACE? YOU LOOK FAMILIAR...

NO TIME TO KID AROUND, PAL! I'M RUNNING A LITTLE LATE TODAY!

CLARK? CLARK KENT?

HI THERE, RON. HOW'S TRICKS?

HUH?

BETTER LOOK BUSY, JIMMY. PERRY'S ALREADY WARNED YOU ABOUT CALLING YOUR GIRLFRIENDS ON THE COMPANY PHONE BILL.

?!

LUCY, YOU'RE NOT GONNA BELIEVE WHO JUST WALKED THROUGH THE DOOR...

HEY, GANG. WHAT'S...

...GOING ...ON?

WHAT'S *UP* WITH EVERYONE TODAY? YOU'RE ALL GAPING AT ME LIKE I'M WEARING MY SHORTS OUTSIDE MY PANTS!

CLARK?

YOU'RE ALIVE! L-LOOK, EVERYBODY! HE'S ALIVE!

WELL, I WAS *LAST* TIME I CHECKED FOR A *PULSE.* WHAT'S THE *GAG,* FOLKS? TONY BEING INVESTIGATED BY THE *HYGIENE BOYS* AGAIN?

OH CLARK, WHERE DID YOU GO? IT'S BEEN *TWELVE MONTHS!*

WHAT?!

I'VE BEEN GONE TWENTY MINUTES AT MOST!

TAKE IT FROM *ME,* SON...

...YOU WALKED OUT THAT DOOR ALMOST A YEAR AGO TO THE DAY, AND NOBODY EVER SAW YOU AGAIN.

YEAH! YOU DIS-APPEARED AROUND THE SAME TIME AS *SUPERMAN,* MR. KENT. WHAT *HAPPENED?*

OH, I GET IT. HAVING *FUN* WITH THE *FARM-BOY,* HUH?

WELL, HOW DO YOU EXPLAIN THE *DATE* ON THE *LATE EDITION,* GUYS?

191

GREAT SCOTT! IT'S...IT'S OFF BY A FULL YEAR!

EASY, KENT. MAYBE YOU'D BETTER TAKE A SEAT.

BUT... HOW COULD I LOSE TWELVE WHOLE MONTHS?

WHO KNOWS?

MAYBE YOU JUST CRACKED UP FOR A WHILE AND WANDERED AROUND IN SOME KINDA DAZE.

HEY, A LOTTA FOLKS WENT BANANAS AFTER SUPERMAN SPLIT!

JIMMY! REALLY!

BUMP!

CLARK, WHAT ABOUT INTERGANG? PERRY AND I FIGURED YOU'D BEEN KILLED BECAUSE YOU WERE GETTING CLOSE TO SOME BIG EXPOSÉ.

COULD THEY HAVE BEEN BEHIND YOUR DISAPPEARANCE?

I DON'T KNOW, LOIS. I DON'T KNOW ANYTHING, EXCEPT THAT I WAS GONE FOR A YEAR! GOD, WHAT HAS THIS DONE TO MY PARENTS?

THEY MUST BE WORRIED SICK ABOUT ME!

UH, SON, I KNOW THIS ISN'T EXACTLY A GOOD TIME...

192

ALL THESE THINGS I CAN DO, ALL THESE POWERS...

MARTHA KENT 1911 - 1996

JONATHAN KENT 1910 - 1996

...AND I COULDN'T EVEN SAVE THEM FROM AN *ORDINARY HOUSE-FIRE*, LANA.

THE ONE TIME THEY *REALLY* NEEDED ME, AND I WASN'T THERE FOR THEM.

YOU SHOULD HAVE SEEN THE *CROWD*, CLARK. PASTOR LINGVIST SAID IT WAS THE *BIGGEST* FUNERAL SMALLVILLE'S EVER HAD.

JONATHAN AND MARTHA WERE VERY SPECIAL PEOPLE.

THANKS FOR BEING HERE TODAY, LANA. I MEAN, CANCELLING YOUR FASHION SHOW AND FLYING ALL THE WAY FROM LOS ANGELES...

NOW THAT MA AND PA ARE *GONE*, YOU'RE THE *ONLY* PERSON I CAN TALK TO ABOUT... *EVERYTHING*.

AW, SHUCKS, METROPOLIS. WHAT ARE BEST FRIENDS FOR?

193

SMALLVILLE CEMETERY

SO... ANY IDEA WHERE YOU WERE DURING THAT MISSING YEAR YET?

WHO *KNOWS?* THE LAST THING I REMEMBER WAS DISPOSING OF S.T.A.R.'S ANTIMATTER ENGINE INTO DEEP SPACE...

THE ONLY EXPLANATION I CAN COME UP WITH IS THAT THE SHOCK WAVE FROM THE EXPLOSION WAS POWERFUL ENOUGH TO PHYSICALLY PROPEL ME TWELVE MONTHS INTO THE FUTURE.

YOU MEAN YOU *JUMPED FORWARD* IN TIME?

EITHER THAT, OR I REALLY *DID* GO NUTS. DID I TELL YOU LOIS AND PERRY FOUND ME A *PSYCHIATRIST?*

I'VE...I'VE LOST *EVERYTHING*, LANA. MY REPUTATION, MY APARTMENT, THE ONLY FAMILY I EVER HAD. EVEN *SUPERGIRL'S* VANISHED.

WHO'D GUESS A SINGLE YEAR COULD MAKE SUCH A *DIFFERENCE?*

194

ROCKETED TO EARTH FROM THE EXPLODING PLANET *KRYPTON*, SUPERMAN ARRIVED HERE MANY YEARS AGO AS THE LONE SURVIVOR OF A DYING WORLD.

ARTIST'S RENDITION

OUR YELLOW SUN AND LIGHTER GRAVITY BLESSED THE MAN OF STEEL WITH FANTASTIC ABILITIES. FOR A TIME, HE USED THESE GIFTS TO FIGHT A NEVER-ENDING BATTLE FOR TRUTH AND JUSTICE.

BUT THE GOOD TIMES COULDN'T LAST FOREVER. SOONER OR LATER, THE FAIRY TALE HAD TO END, AND ONE DAY, OUT OF THE BLUE, OUR HERO *VANISHED*, LEAVING THE SKIES EMPTY ONCE AGAIN.

TODAY MARKS THE FIRST ANNIVERSARY OF THE MAN OF TOMORROW'S DISAPPEARANCE. TONIGHT, *METROPOLIS EDITION* ASKS HOW WE'VE FARED IN SUPERMAN'S ABSENCE ... ONE YEAR LATER.

ONE YEAR LATER

195

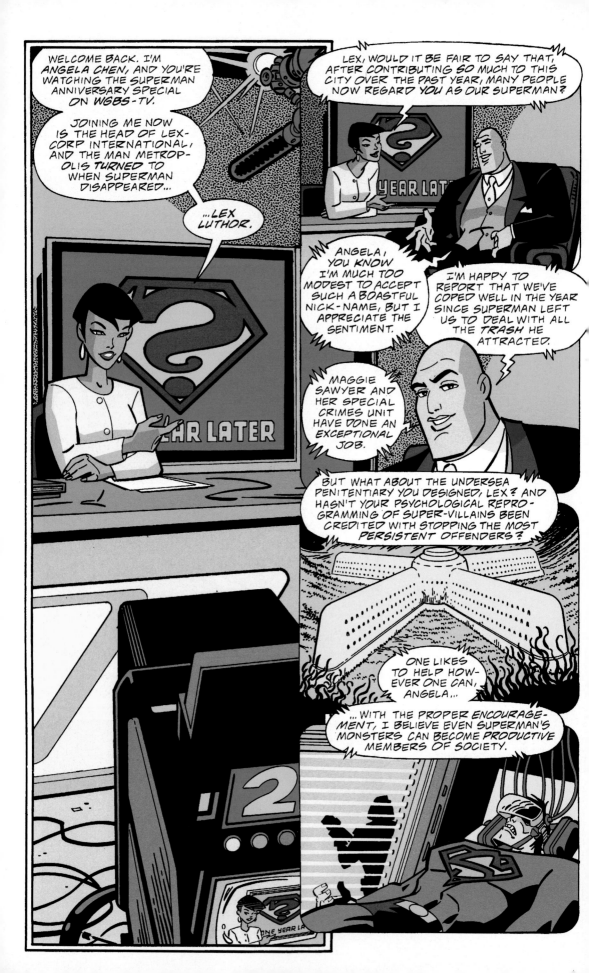

WELCOME BACK. I'M ANGELA CHEN, AND YOU'RE WATCHING THE SUPERMAN ANNIVERSARY SPECIAL ON *WGBS-TV.*

JOINING ME NOW IS THE HEAD OF LEX-CORP INTERNATIONAL, AND THE MAN METROP-OLIS *TURNED* TO WHEN SUPERMAN DISAPPEARED...

...LEX LUTHOR.

LEX, WOULD IT BE FAIR TO SAY THAT, AFTER CONTRIBUTING *SO* MUCH TO THIS CITY OVER THE PAST YEAR, MANY PEOPLE NOW REGARD *YOU* AS OUR SUPERMAN?

ANGELA, YOU *KNOW* I'M MUCH TOO MODEST TO ACCEPT SUCH A BOASTFUL NICK-NAME, BUT I APPRECIATE THE SENTIMENT.

I'M HAPPY TO REPORT THAT WE'VE COPED WELL IN THE YEAR SINCE SUPERMAN LEFT US TO DEAL WITH ALL THE *TRASH* HE ATTRACTED.

MAGGIE SAWYER AND HER SPECIAL CRIMES UNIT HAVE DONE AN EXCEPTIONAL JOB.

BUT WHAT ABOUT THE UNDERSEA PENITENTIARY YOU DESIGNED, LEX? AND HASN'T YOUR PSYCHOLOGICAL REPRO-GRAMMING OF SUPER-VILLAINS BEEN CREDITED WITH STOPPING THE MOST PERSISTENT OFFENDERS?

ONE LIKES TO HELP HOW-EVER ONE CAN, ANGELA...

...WITH THE PROPER ENCOURAGE-MENT, I BELIEVE EVEN SUPERMAN'S MONSTERS CAN BECOME *PRODUCTIVE* MEMBERS OF SOCIETY.

BETWEEN FIGHTING CRIME, WORKING TOWARDS DEVELOPING A CANCER VACCINE AND MAKING HUGE FINANCIAL CONTRIBUTIONS TOWARD THIRD WORLD DEBT, YOU'VE KEPT YOURSELF PRETTY BUSY THIS YEAR, HAVEN'T YOU?

AND LET'S NOT FORGET THE NOBEL PRIZE LEX-S.T.A.R. PICKED UP FOR SOLVING THE ENERGY CRISIS WITH YOUR ANTI-MATTER ENGINE.

HAS LEX LUTHOR FINALLY BLOSSOMED NOW THAT THE MAN OF STEEL IS NO LONGER CASTING A SHADOW OVER HIM?

ANGELA, IF YOU'LL FORGIVE ME...

...BUT I THINK YOU'RE EXAGGERATING SUPERMAN'S IMPORTANCE.

MANKIND FUNCTIONED PERFECTLY WELL AS A SPECIES BEFORE HE DAZZLED US WITH HIS WIDESCREEN THEATRICS...

...AND WE'RE DOING PERFECTLY WELL WITH-OUT HIM.

WHAT'S WRONG, KAL-EL?

TROUBLED BECAUSE YOU WENT MISSING FOR A YEAR... OR BECAUSE THEY WERE CAPABLE OF SURVIVING IN YOUR ABSENCE?

WHO...?

SOMEONE WHO'S TRAVELLED A GREAT DISTANCE TO BE HERE.

I WAS WORRIED WE WERE WRONG AT FIRST, BUT MY INSTRUMENTS SUGGEST EVERY ATOM IN YOUR BODY IS GENUINELY KRYPTONIAN.

THERE CAN BE NO MISTAKE, AFTER ALL...

GOOD GOD...!

MY NAME IS LARA, WIFE OF JOR-EL, AND AFTER ALL THESE YEARS, I'VE FINALLY FOUND MY MISSING CHILD.

THIS... THIS IS IMPOSSIBLE! MY MOTHER'S DEAD!

SHE DIED WITH EVERYONE ELSE ON KRYPTON!

KRYPTON WAS A RACE OF GENIUSES, MY SON.

DO YOU REALLY THINK A BILLION YEARS OF SCIENTIFIC EXCELLENCE COULD BE ERADICATED BY A FORCE AS CRUDE AS NATURE?

OUR WORLD WAS DESTROYED, ITS PIECES SCATTERED ACROSS THE COSMOS, BUT YOUR FATHER SAVED ONE OF OUR GREATEST CITIES, KAL-EL.

YOUR BIRTHPLACE LIVES ON. KRYPTONOPOLIS HAS SURVIVED.

YOU'RE...YOU'RE LYING! THIS IS A TRICK...!

EXAMINE MY BODY WITH YOUR ENHANCED VISION, CHILD.

CAN'T YOU SEE THE SIMILARITIES WE SHARE IN TERMS OF BASIC CELL STRUCTURE, BLOOD TYPE AND D.N.A. PATTERNS?

I'VE COME TO TAKE YOU HOME, KAL-EL.

YOUR FATHER ACHES TO SEE HIS BELOVED SON AGAIN.

POOR CRITTER...

THE COMPUTER WHICH ORGANIZED THEIR FEEDING TIMES MUST HAVE MAL-FUNCTIONED WHILE I WAS GONE. ALL THE BEASTS IN MY ALIEN SANCTUARY STARVED TO DEATH.

I UNDERSTAND YOUR PETS AREN'T ALL YOU'VE LOST LATELY...

YOUR "CLARK KENT" IDENTITY, SUPERMAN, EVERYTHING THAT ANCHORED YOU TO THIS ROCK, HAS BEEN DESTABILIZED SINCE YOU DISAPPEARED.

PERHAPS THE COSMIC MISTAKE THAT CAUSED YOU TO BE RAISED IN THIS BACKWARD JUNGLE HAS SIMPLY RECTIFIED IT-SELF, KAL-EL.

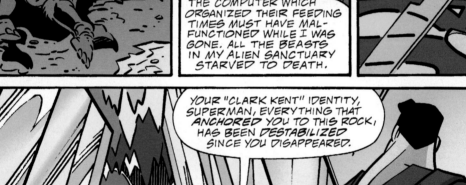

THE ONLY SENSIBLE THING TO DO NOW...

...IS COME HOME.

200

LOOK, ABOUT WHAT YOU SAID BACK THERE... I'VE GOT *RESPONSIBILITIES* HERE. MY POWERS MEAN IT'S MY *DUTY* TO HELP THOSE WHO CAN'T HELP THEM-SELVES.

YOU WERE MISSING FOR A *WHOLE YEAR* AND THEY BARELY NOTICED, MY SON. IF ANYTHING, IT'S HAD A *POSITIVE* EFFECT ON THEIR CULTURE.

I SUSPECT THEY WERE BECOMING A LITTLE *TOO* RELIANT ON THEIR SUPER-HUMAN *BABYSITTER.*

STILL, I MUST ADMIT, LEAVING THESE ABILITIES BEHIND IS GOING TO BE PAINFUL.

WE'RE ACTUALLY HAVING A *CONVERSATION,* DESPITE BEING MORE THAN TWO MILES APART. IT'S *ASTONISHING...*

"FLIGHT, SPEED, TELE-SCOPIC VISION..."

"IF WE FOCUS, WE CAN EVEN SEE THROUGH *WALLS...*"

201

KAL-EL, I'VE FOUND THE EARTH FEMALE YOU WERE SEARCHING FOR.

I KNOW, MOTHER. I CAN SEE HER FROM HERE.

BUT I THOUGHT YOU WANTED TO TELL THIS LOIS LANE HOW YOU FELT ABOUT HER BEFORE WE TELEPORTED BACK TO KRYPTONOPOLIS.

DIDN'T YOU SUSPECT THE THE TWO OF YOU HAD A FUTURE TOGETHER AS A PAIRING?

TIMES CHANGE, MOTHER.

THE RING SHE WEARS ON HER LEFT HAND HOLDS SOME SIGNIFICANCE, DOESN'T IT? THESE ALIEN CUSTOMS ARE SO PERPLEXING...

IS IT A SIGN OF RECENT BEREAVEMENT?

SOMETHING LIKE THAT.

COME ON-- LET'S GO HOME.

202

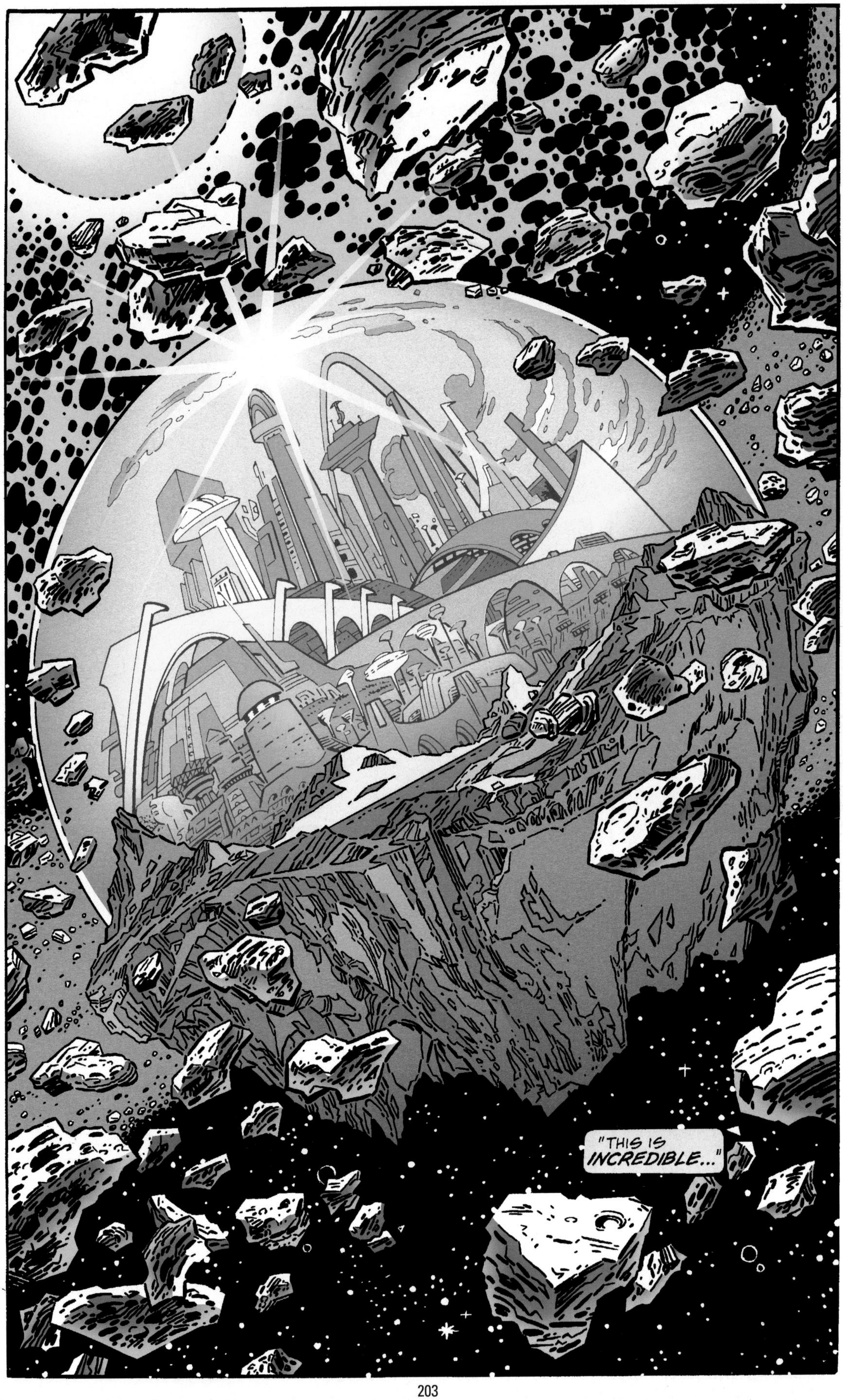
"THIS IS INCREDIBLE..."

I'VE EXPLORED KRYPTONOPOLIS BEFORE USING BRAINIAC'S SIMULATOR, BUT WORDS CAN'T *DESCRIBE* ACTUALLY *BEING* HERE IN THE FLESH.

THIS IS UNLIKE ANYTHING I'VE EVER EXPERIENCED.

BRAINIAC IS *ALIVE?*

YES. HE SHOWED UP ON EARTH A WHILE AGO, BUT I TOOK CARE OF HIM BEFORE HE DID ANY SERIOUS DAMAGE.

I'M PROBABLY AS FAMILIAR WITH THE STREETS OF KRYPTONOPOLIS AS SOME OF THE PEOPLE LIVING HERE.

THE DATA HE STOLE FROM KRYPTON IS KEPT AT MY FORTRESS AS A PERMANENT *REFERENCE* OF MY KRYPTONIAN HERITAGE.

OH, I'M SURE WE STILL HAVE *SOME* SURPRISES FOR YOU, KAL.

204

THIS IS WHERE YOUR FATHER REGULATES EVERYTHING, FROM THE COLOR OF THE SKY TO THE DIRECTION OF THE WIND IN OUR GREAT CITY...

...AS HE SCANS THE DEPTHS OF SPACE FOR A SUITABLE PLANET, WHERE WE MIGHT RELOCATE AND START AFRESH.

INCREDIBLE...

ONE MAN'S INGENUITY SAVING AN ENTIRE POPULATION LIKE THIS...IT'S AWE-INSPIRING, MOTHER. I CAN'T WAIT TO MEET HIM.

WELL, THERE'S NO TIME LIKE THE PRESENT.

FATHER...?

YOU...

...YOU TREACHEROUS WITCH!

WASN'T IT ENOUGH THAT YOU CORRUPTED KRYPTON'S LAST SURVIVING COLONY WITH YOUR INSANE IDEAS? MUST THIS POOR DEVIL DIE TOO?

WHAT ARE YOU TALKING ABOUT-- ≶UNNHH!≷

YOU CAN EXPLAIN THE DETAILS, MY REBELLIOUS HUSBAND.

WAK!

I'M TIRED OF LISTENING TO THIS ONE'S IRRITATING EARTH ACCENT.

205

CAN'T SAY I'M *SURPRISED*. WHO-EVER YOU ARE, I SUSPECTED YOU WERE BEHIND MY MISSING YEAR, SO I PLAYED ALONG TO FIND OUT WHAT YOU WANTED OR WHERE YOU CAME FROM.

WE *ARE* YOUR PARENTS, SUPERMAN. THE TRUTH IS, NO ONE KNOWS WHERE *YOU* CAME FROM...

MY INSANE WIFE AND HER SURVEILLANCE TEAM BELIEVE YOU WERE SOMEHOW CAUGHT IN A MASSIVE *ANTIMATTER* EXPLOSION FROM ANOTHER DIMENSION...

...A DIMENSION WHERE I *FAILED* TO SAVE KRYPTON'S CAPITAL, AND THESE INGRATES *PERISHED* WITH THE REST OF OUR PLANET.

LARA LURED YOU HERE BECAUSE YOUR PRESENCE WAS AN *UNEXPECTED FACTOR* IN HER INVASION PLANS AND NEEDED TO BE DEALT WITH.

SHE COULD AFFORD NO POSSIBILITY OF FAILURE.

WAIT-- *INVASION PLANS?*

NATURALLY. WHY SHOULD A HIGHER FORM OF LIFE CLING TO SOME *METEORITE* WHEN THEY CAN LIVE LIKE *GODS* UNDER A *YELLOW SUN?*

WE'VE SET *OUR* SIGHTS ON *EARTH!*

BUT...IF I'M IN ANOTHER DIMENSION, THE SUPERMAN AND SUPERGIRL OF *THIS* REALITY ARE STILL OUT THERE SOMEWHERE!

HE AND SUPER-GIRL CAN STILL FIND A WAY TO *STOP* YOU!

REALLY...?

206

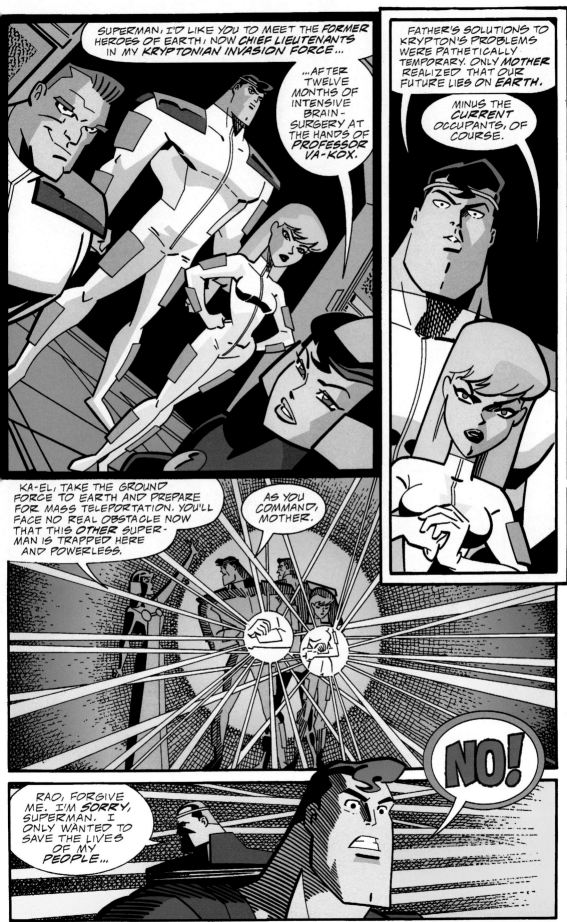

SUPERMAN, I'D LIKE YOU TO MEET THE *FORMER* HEROES OF EARTH, NOW *CHIEF LIEUTENANTS* IN MY *KRYPTONIAN INVASION FORCE*...

...AFTER TWELVE MONTHS OF INTENSIVE BRAIN-SURGERY AT THE HANDS OF *PROFESSOR VA-KOX.*

FATHER'S SOLUTIONS TO KRYPTON'S PROBLEMS WERE PATHETICALLY TEMPORARY. ONLY *MOTHER* REALIZED THAT OUR FUTURE LIES ON *EARTH.*

MINUS THE *CURRENT* OCCUPANTS, OF COURSE.

KA-EL, TAKE THE GROUND FORCE TO EARTH AND PREPARE FOR MASS TELEPORTATION. YOU'LL FACE NO REAL OBSTACLE NOW THAT THIS *OTHER* SUPER-MAN IS TRAPPED HERE AND POWERLESS.

AS YOU COMMAND, MOTHER.

NO!

RAO, FORGIVE ME. I'M *SORRY*, SUPERMAN. I ONLY WANTED TO SAVE THE LIVES OF MY *PEOPLE*...

"...BUT IT SEEMS I'VE DOOMED EARTH IN THE PROCESS."

TO BE CONTINUED!

208

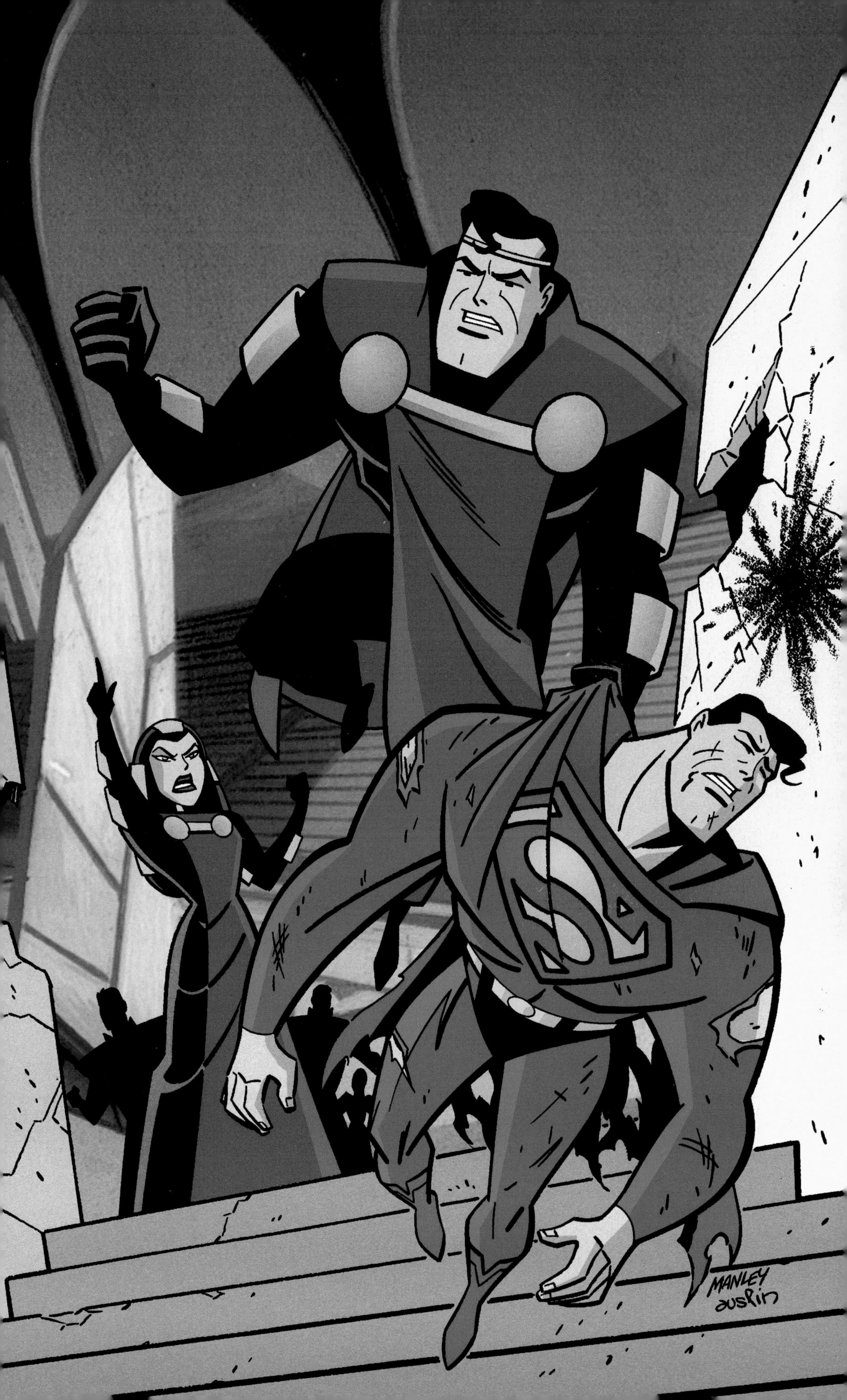
MANLEY
austin

FAMILY REUNION
PART TWO

ET - DAILY P

ARREST ME, YOU COWARDS!

LET'S SEE THE SPECIAL CRIMES UNIT WORK UP A LITTLE SWEAT FOR THEIR WAGES!

MARK MILLAR
WRITER
ALUIR AMANCIO
PENCILLER
TERRY AUSTIN
INKER
PHIL FELIX
LETTERER
MARIE SEVERIN
COLORIST
ZYLONOL
SEPARATIONS
FRANK BERRIOS
ASSISTANT EDITOR
MIKE McAVENNIE
EDITOR

SUPERMAN
CREATED BY
JERRY SIEGEL &
JOE SHUSTER

WE MIGHT AS WELL BE FIRING *PEANUTS*, CAPTAIN SAWYER!

THIS *PROFESSOR VA-KOX* IS AS STRONG AS SUPERMAN EVER WAS!

FALL BACK, PEOPLE! HE'S COMING IN FOR THE *KILL!*

RESISTANCE IS USELESS!

THRUNNCH!

KRYPTON SHALL CONQUER *ALL*, AND EVEN YOUR GREATEST HEROES, *SUPERMAN* AND *SUPERGIRL*, NOW TOIL UNDER *OUR* COMMAND!

THE PEOPLE OF *KRYPTONOPOLIS* CHOOSE EARTH AS THEIR NEW *HOME*...

...AND METROPOLIS WILL BE REBUILT AS OUR GLORIOUS NEW *CAPITAL!*

SSSSSs

THUNK!

THE KRYPTONIANS ARE GETTING *CLOSER*, LEX...

WE CAN'T *HANG ON* ANY LONGER! YOU'VE GOT TO GET IN THE CHOPPER BEFORE IT'S *TOO LATE!*

I'M NOT GOING *ANYWHERE*, MERCY.

I'VE PLOWED *TOO MUCH* INTO METROPOLIS OVER THE YEARS TO BE ROBBED OF MY DESTINY BY A *BRAINWASHED MAN OF STEEL.*

YOU CAN RUN IF YOU WANT TO...

...BUT *LEX LUTHOR* MOVES FOR NEITHER MAN *NOR SUPERMAN.*

I PLAN TO STAY HERE AND *FIGHT.*

"YOU SHOULD CONSIDER YOUR-SELF *FORTUNATE,* SUPERMAN.

"BEING HURLED BY AN *ANTIMATTER BLAST* INTO A DIMENSION WHERE KRYPTONOPOLIS *SURVIVED* KRYPTON'S EXPLOSION ALLOWED YOU A CHANCE TO WITNESS A GREAT MOMENT IN YOUR *HOMEWORLD'S* HISTORY..."

UNFORTUNATELY, YOU MUST REMAIN *TRAPPED* HERE UNDER A RED SUN WITH MY REBELLIOUS HUSBAND, *JOR-EL,* WHILE MY LANDING PARTY PREPARES EARTH FOR OUR INVASION.

THERE'S NO NEED TO *GLOAT,* LARA.

YOU MAY HAVE CAPTURED *US,* BUT THERE'S *STILL* A CHANCE THE HEROES OF THIS DIMENSION WILL CHANGE THEIR MINDS!

SUPERMAN AND SUPERGIRL? DON'T *DELUDE* YOURSELF...

EARTH'S CHAMPIONS OBEY OUR EVERY *COMMAND* AFTER A YEAR OF INTENSIVE *BRAIN SURGERY* AT THE HANDS OF *PROFESSOR VA-KOX.*

BETTER KNOWN NOW AS *LIEUTENANTS KAL-EL* AND *KARA...*

...THEY'RE THE MOST ENTHUSIASTIC SUPPORTERS OF MY NEW ORDER.

"JOR-EL'S GENIUS SAVED US WHEN THE REST OF KRYPTON *DIED*, SUPERMAN, BUT THIS IS A *VOLATILE* LITTLE ROCK WE CLING TO."

"THE TERRIBLE YEARS WE SPENT RE-BUILDING OUR SOCIETY HAVE EXTER-MINATED ANY *SQUEAMISHNESS* WE MIGHT HAVE HAD ABOUT *DOMINATING* AN INFERIOR SPECIES."

THIS PHILOSOPHY WILL BECOME CLEARER TO YOU AFTER THE BRAIN SURGERY.

WHY DON'T YOU JUST *KILL* US, YOU ANIMAL?

KILL ANOTHER *KRYPTONIAN?* WE'RE NOT *SAVAGES*, SUPERMAN.

KILLING HUMANS LIKE THE KENTS MEANS *NOTHING*, BUT MURDERING ANOTHER INTELLIGENT LIFE-FORM IS COMPLETELY *BARBARIC.*

THEY...

...THEY TOLD ME MA AND PA DIED IN A *FIRE*...

QUITE TRUE, MY FRIEND, BUT WHO DO YOU THINK STARTED THE FIRE WITH HER *HEAT VISION?* IT MADE KAL-EL AND KARA MORE SUSCEP-TIBLE TO THEIR SURGERY.

LIVING AMONG HUMANS HAS MADE YOU SO NAIVE.

MURDERERRR!!

FZAAK!

OH, SUPERMAN, I DIDN'T REALIZE YOU WERE ALSO *SQUEAMISH.*

YOU SHOULD SEE WHAT THE LANDING PARTY IS DOING TO *METROPOLIS.*

215

I'M IMPRESSED WITH THE AMORALITY YOU EMPLOY TO CARRY OUT YOUR INSTRUCTIONS, LIEUTENANT KARA.

FWOOM!

IT MAKES THE HAIRS ON MY NECK STAND ON END TO KNOW MY NEUROSURGERY CAN CAUSE SUCH DRAMATIC REVERSALS IN CHARACTER!

WE HAVE TO DEMOLISH THESE PRIMITIVE STRUCTURES IF WE'RE TO BUILD A WORLD FIT FOR KRYPTONIANS, PROFESSOR VA-KOX.

LOOK AT THEM TRY TO DEFY US BY FLEEING THE CITY!

DON'T THESE MAGGOTS REALIZE WE'RE GOING TO NEED THEM AS SLAVES WHEN WE RULE THE WORLD?

SUPERMAN! NO...!

CHOOM!

216

HUH?

HIM NOT SUPERMAN ANYMORE, LOIS!

THAT WHY *BIZARRO* HAVE TO SAVE METROPOLIS NOW!

THE METAL MAN SAVED US, MOMMY! HE *SAVED* US!

DON'T LOOK SO SURPRISED, LANE. WE MIGHT BE *CRIMINALS,* BUT WE'RE NOT *MONSTERS!*

A CHOICE BETWEEN *HIDING IN OUR CELLS* AND DEFENDING METROPOLIS REALLY WASN'T SUCH A HARD ONE TO MAKE.

BRAVE WORDS, METALLO.

LET'S PUT THEM TO THE *TEST.*

217

THREE AGAINST TWO AIN'T *FAIR*, SUPES!

LET'S EVEN THE *ODDS* A LITTLE AND GIVE THOSE BOYS A *CHANCE*, HUH?

THANK *LUTHOR* FOR THIS TACTICAL *MASTERSTROKE*, VA-KOX!

≡AAAIGGH!≡

THE *PARASITE!*

KAPOW!

YEAH! WHO *BETTER* TO FACE OFF THREE *SUPER-PEOPLE* THAN THE *JAILBIRDS* WHO FIGHT DUDES OF STEEL ALL THE TIME!

THWACK

≡UNNGH!≡

HOORAY! YAAYY!

HUH? WHY AM EVERYONE STILL CHEERING EVIL SUPERMAN?

THEY'RE CHEERING US, YOU FOOL! DON'T YOU GET IT?

WE'RE *HEROES* NOW, MAN...!

A SHAME YOU'LL BE REMEMBERED *POSTHUMOUSLY!*

POW!

WHAMM!

MAYBE WE'LL ERECT A *STATUE* IN YOUR HONOR WHEN THIS IS *ALL OVER*, YOU MISERABLE *INSECTS!*

"YOUR PEOPLE OUT THERE ARE EXCITED BECAUSE THEY THINK THEY'RE ABOUT TO BECOME *SUPERHUMAN* TOMORROW..."

"...BUT HAVE THEY REALLY *STOPPED* TO CONSIDER THE *CONSEQUENCES?*"

ARE YOU *HONESTLY* PREPARED TO ROB *FIVE BILLION PEOPLE* OF THEIR WORLD JUST SO YOU CAN FLY AND SEE THROUGH WALLS?

YOU'RE WASTING YOUR TIME, SUPERMAN. HE CAN'T EVEN *HEAR* YOU.

ALL OUR GUARD IS THINKING ABOUT IS WHICH EARTH CITY HE'S GOING TO TAKE ONCE HE'S ERASED THE *PRESENT* POPULATION.

HOW CAN YOU JUST *STAND THERE,* JOR-EL? YOU SOUND LIKE YOU DON'T EVEN CARE ANYMORE!

OH, I *CARE,* SUPERMAN. A SCIENTIST HONORS *ALL* FORMS OF LIFE.

WHY *ELSE* WOULD I HAVE WORKED SO HARD TO SAVE A CITY AS *COLD* AND *DESPICABLE* AS KRYPTONOPOLIS HAS *BECOME?*

219

DO YOU THINK KRYPTON EXPLODING IS WHAT DROVE THEM *MAD*?

UNQUESTIONABLY, BUT EVEN MADNESS CAN'T EXCUSE LARA'S TERRIBLE PLAN TO SAVE A CITY BY EXTERMINATING AN ENTIRE *WORLD*!

MY ONLY DREAM AS I REBUILT THIS PLACE WAS THAT ONE DAY I'D FIND MY *SON* AGAIN, AND WE'D ALL LIVE TOGETHER IN PERFECT HARMONY.

I SEE NOW THAT I WAS FOOLING MYSELF ALL ALONG.

SAVING KRYPTONOPOLIS WAS A *MAJOR* MISCALCULATION.

BZZT!

I HOPE YOU KNOW HOW TO FIGHT, SUPERMAN.

MERCIFUL RAO! THE SHIELD'S DOWN!

I'VE BEEN IN A COUPLE OF SCRAPES!

WHOKK!

220

...SO IF THIS *OTHER* KAL-EL CAME FROM ANOTHER DIMENSION, WHAT DO YOU THINK HAPPENED TO THE KRYPTON OVER THERE?

I'M NOT SURE, BUT HE OBVIOUSLY DIDN'T HAVE TO STRUGGLE LIKE *WE* DID.

JUST *LOOK* AT HIM-- HE'S *SOFT*, LIKE JOR-EL. HE WAS PROBABLY *SPOILED* BACK THERE, AND SEES HIS EARTH AS SOME SORT OF *PET* TO PROTECT!

CONSIDER YOURSELF *LUCKY* I DON'T TELL YOU HOW "EASY" *MY* KRYPTON HAD IT, FRIEND!

WAK!

WOK!

YOU TAKE CARE OF EARTH. LEAVE KRYPTONOPOLIS TO *ME*.

JUST *CURIOUS*-- HOW DID YOU KNOW HOW TO DISABLE THE LASER-SHIELD BACK THERE?

WHO DO YOU THINK *DESIGNED* THE ORIGINAL SYSTEM?

LET'S GO. WE'VE GOT TO GET YOU A TELEPORTER DEVICE AS QUICKLY AS POSSIBLE.

WAIT, JOR-EL...

I UNDERSTAND YOU *AREN'T* MY REAL FATHER... THAT I'M HERE IN ANOTHER DIMENSION... BUT...

I KNOW, KAL. I KNOW...

...I FEEL *EXACTLY* THE SAME WAY.

COME ON... *SON*...

"...LET'S GET TO WORK."

AARGH!

FUNNY, ISN'T IT, METALLO? IF THE PARASITE HADN'T *DRAINED* SOME OF KAL-EL'S POWERS, YOUR *KRYPTONITE HEART* WOULD NEVER HAVE AFFECTED HIM.

HE'D PROBABLY *KICK* HIMSELF IF HE HAD THE CHANCE.

HOLD METALLO *STEADY,* KARA! WE CAN'T GET TOO CLOSE!

AARRGHH!

YOU FORGET I'M FROM *ARGO,* PROFESSOR. MY WORLD DIED BECAUSE KRYPTON'S EXPLOSION KNOCKED US OUT OF OUR ORBIT...

...BUT THE RADIATION THAT'S DEADLY TO YOU MEANS *NOTHING* TO ME, MEANING I CAN *TOUCH, SCRAMBLE* OR *POACH* THIS STUPID ROCK!

S-SUPERGIRL... PLEASE... DON'T *DO* THI--

LET'S SEE HOW *SCARY* YOU ARE *WITHOUT* YOUR POWER SUPPLY, METALLO!

EXCELLENT, LIEUTENANT KARA.

NOW, WHERE IS THIS *LEX LUTHOR* WHO THINKS HE CAN MATCH WITS WITH HIS *SUPERIORS?*

222

OVER *HERE*, PROFESSOR! FORMING A LINE WITH THE *OTHER* RATS!

I THINK THEY'RE TRYING TO SAY THIS IS AS FAR AS WE GO!

HOW *DARE* YOU TRY TO COMMAND ME, YOU FILTHY LITTLE ANIMAL?!

HOW *DARE* YOU EVEN LOOK ME IN THE EYE?!

YOU'RE NOT THE *FIRST* KRYPTONIAN I'VE STARED DOWN, PROFESSOR VA-KOX, AND YOU WON'T BE THE *LAST!* DO YOUR WORST!

IMPUDENT FOOL! I'LL USE THAT HEAD AS A WRECKING BALL...!

GREAT CAESAR'S GHOST!

LOOK! UP IN THE SKY!

IT'S A BIRD! IT'S A PLANE!

IT'S *HIM.* IT'S *REALLY* HIM...

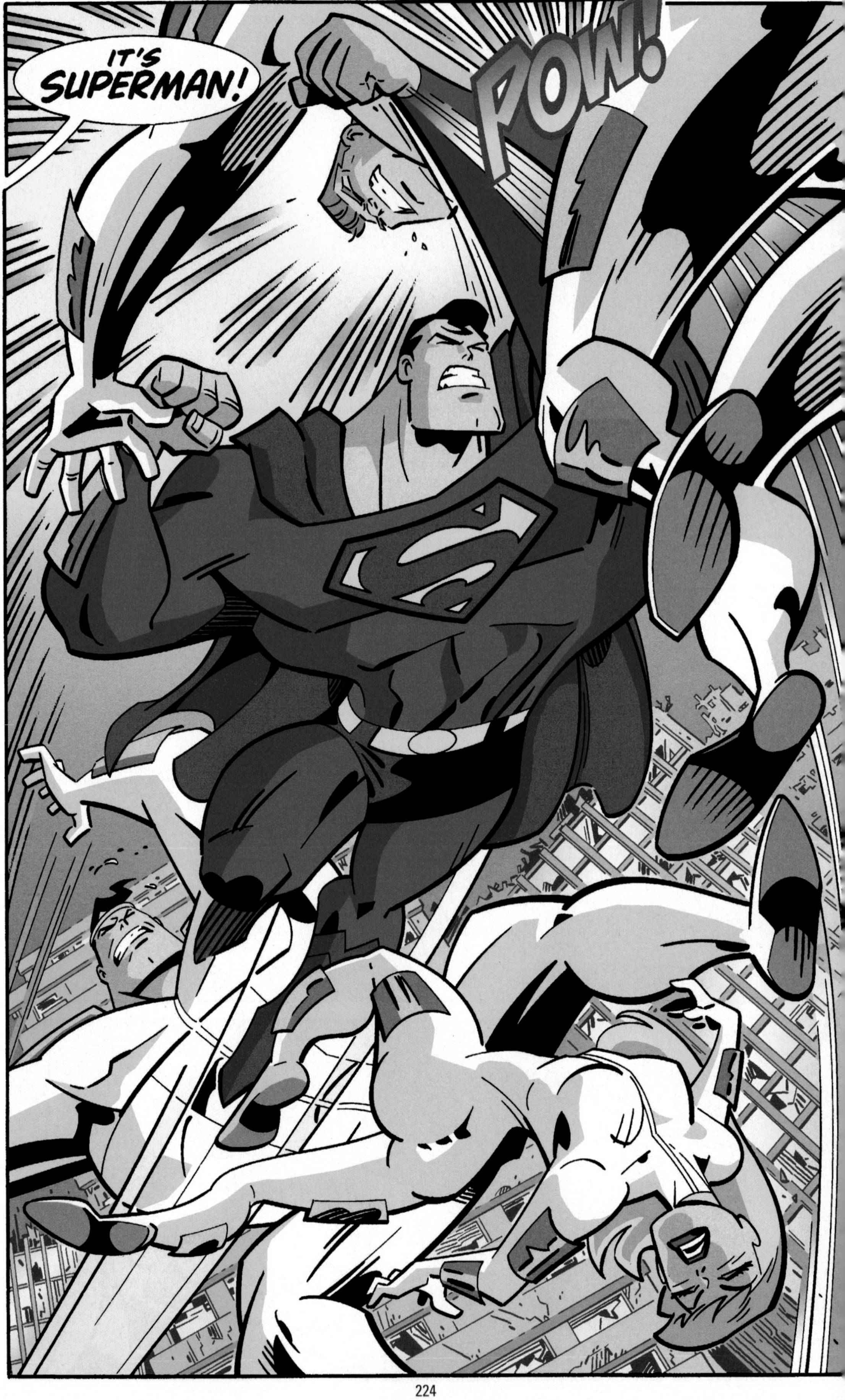
IT'S SUPERMAN!
POW!

S-SUPERMAN!?

HE MUST HAVE TELEPORTED HERE! BUT HOW DID HE ESCAPE?

WHO CARES? GET AFTER HIM! NOTHING MUST JEOPARDIZE LARA'S INVASION PLANS!

DO YOU REALIZE YOU'RE TAKING ORDERS FROM THE MEN AND WOMEN WHO MURDERED YOUR ADOPTIVE PARENTS?

HUH?

WHAMM!

UNNH!

NO MATTER WHAT THEY TOLD YOU, THE KENTS DIDN'T DIE IN A FIRE! YOUR GLORIOUS LEADER EXECUTED THEM WITH HER HEAT VISION!

KRAK!

SHOULD IT?

DOESN'T THAT MEAN ANYTHING TO EITHER OF YOU?

225

I THINK SUPERMAN HOPED THE NEWS THAT THE KENTS WERE MURDERED WOULD SOMEHOW BRING ABOUT A KIND OF *REHABILITATION,* KAL-EL.

OBVIOUSLY, HE DOESN'T REALIZE THE PROFESSOR TAUGHT US TO *IGNORE* OUR HUMAN CONSCIENCES AND BECOME THE *SUPERIOR* BEINGS WE WERE *BORN* TO BE.

YOU MEAN *SHOCK* US INTO SEEING THE *"ERROR OF OUR WAYS"*?

IS HE REALLY *THAT* NAIVE?

I THOUGHT... WHEN *HE* SHOWED UP, I HOPED...

THIS ISN'T LOOKING *GOOD,* PEOPLE.

ENOUGH *TALKING,* YOU TWO.

TIME TO ELIMINATE THE OPPOSITION, I THINK.

≡HNN≡ OKAY, JOR-EL-- NOW!

FLAASH!

GREAT MOONS OF KRYPTON! WHERE--?

BACK WHERE YOU CAN'T DO ANY HARM, VA-KOX!

HAVE YOU *LOST* YOUR MIND, JOR-EL? ALL WE HAVE TO DO IS TELEPORT BACK TO EARTH AND FINISH WHAT WE *STARTED*, YOU IMBECILE!

OOF!

ONLY IF THE TELEPORTER IS STILL OPERATIONAL...

WHAT ARE YOU TALKING ABOUT?

THE PLAN WAS THAT I HAD TO BRING YOU BACK HERE WHILE JOR-EL SABOTAGED THE TRANS-PORTER. YOU MIGHT FIGURE OUT HOW TO BUILD ONE YOUR-SELF. *SOMEDAY*, VA-KOX, BUT NOT FOR AWHILE.

IS THIS *TRUE*, JOR-EL?

NOT...NOT EVEN *CLOSE*, LARA.

I'M *SORRY*, SUPERMAN, BUT I'M AFRAID I *RENEGED* ON OUR PLAN.

227

WHAT...?

CONGRATULATIONS, HUSBAND.

DOES THIS MEAN YOU'VE *FINALLY* COME TO YOUR SENSES, AND OUR INVASION MEETS WITH YOUR *APPROVAL*?

DON'T BE RIDICULOUS.

I DECIDED TO DEVOTE MY ATTENTIONS TO FINDING A WAY TO TELEPORT SUPERMAN BACK HOME TO HIS *OWN* DIMENSION INSTEAD.

IT WAS AN UNFORTUNATE QUIRK OF FATE THAT BROUGHT HIM HERE...

...AND IT'S ONLY *RIGHT* HE SHOULD BE SPARED WHAT COMES NEXT.

HOW *MAGNANIMOUS* OF YOU, JOR-EL... BUT IT SEEMS YOU'VE FORGOTTEN SUPERMAN REACHED US VIA AN *ANTIMATTER* EXPLOSION.

TELEPORTING HIM BACK WOULD REQUIRE EVERY *ERG* OF ENERGY WE HAVE IN KRYPTONOPOLIS!

PRECISELY, "DARLING." ALL I HAVE TO DO NOW IS PRESS THIS BUTTON, AND EVERYTHING THAT KEEPS THIS WRETCHED CITY ALIVE WILL BE PUT TO A MUCH BETTER USE.

Y-YOU MEAN YOU PLAN TO *DESTROY* KRYPTONOPOLIS?

KRYPTONOPOLIS WAS *DOOMED* THE MOMENT YOU DECIDED FIVE BILLION LIVES COULD BE SACRIFICED FOR HUNDREDS, VA-KOX.

I'D RATHER SEE THIS ROCK DIE THAN LET YOU *MONSTERS* MURDER AN INNOCENT WORLD LIKE *EARTH*.

228

NO, JOR-EL! THERE MUST BE ANOTHER WAY--!

DON'T GO ANY CLOSER, YOU FOOL! HE'LL KILL US ALL!

I'M SORRY I *DECEIVED* YOU, SUPERMAN, BUT I HAD NO CHOICE.

IF EVER PROOF WAS NEEDED THAT KRYPTON'S CAPITAL SHOULD HAVE DIED WITH THE REST OF OUR WORLD, SURELY *THIS* WAS IT.

YOU FAILED TO SAVE KRYPTON, HUSBAND, AND THIS IS SOMETHING THAT, I CONCEDE, OUR POPULATION HAS NEVER RECOVERED FROM...

...BUT I BEG YOU TO RECONSIDER ENDING THIS SANCTUARY IT HAS TAKEN US YEARS TO BUILD!

I-I ONLY WANTED WHAT WAS BEST FOR MY PEOPLE! IF THAT MEANT CRUSHING THE EARTH TRASH, THEN SO BE IT!

ARE YOU SERIOUSLY SUGGESTING THAT THOSE *PATHETIC ANTS* DESERVE THAT BEAUTIFUL WORLD MORE THAN THEIR *GENETIC MASTERS*?

IS THAT WHAT YOU'RE *HONESTLY* SAYING TO ME?!

I THINK YOU'VE JUST ANSWERED YOUR OWN QUESTION, LARA...

KLIK!

229

CHOOM!

MOONS OF KRYPTON!

MY GOD! I...I'M FADING AWAY!

YOUR TRANSPORTER ACTIVATED WHEN I TRIGGERED THE EXPLOSION. YOU'LL BE SHIELDED FROM THE BLAST.

WE'VE BEEN HERE ONCE BEFORE, SUPERMAN. YOU BEING SENT TO A BETTER LIFE, WHILE EVERYTHING THAT WAS KRYPTON DIES.

MAKE ME AS PROUD AS I WAS THE FIRST TIME.

S-STOP THIS, JOR-EL! IT'S NOT TOO LATE!

GOODBYE, MY SON...

"...MAY RAO ALWAYS BE THERE TO GUIDE YOU."

GOOD LORD!

PROFESSOR, WHAT'S WRONG?

N-NOTHING, MY DEAR. IT JUST LOOKED LIKE SUPERMAN ... DISAPPEARED FOR A MOMENT IN THE BLAST OF THE ANTI-MATTER ENGINE.

ANOTHER DIMENSION?

WHAT ARE YOU TALKING ABOUT, PROFESSOR? THE BLAST SENT ME INTO ANOTHER DIMENSION FOR AT LEAST A WEEK!

SORRY, SUPER-MAN, BUT YOU ONLY DISAPPEARED FOR A FRACTION OF A SECOND. PERHAPS THE BLAST KNOCKED YOU UN-CONSCIOUS FOR AN INSTANT, AND CAUSED YOU TO HALLUCINATE.

MAYBE.

IF YOU'LL EXCUSE ME, PROFESSOR HAMILTON --

"-- THERE'S SOMETHING I REALLY HAVE TO CHECK."

THIS WORLD YOU THINK YOU LEFT BEHIND, CLARK... DO YOU THINK IT'S GOING TO COPE WITHOUT A SUPERMAN?

WELL, IT SEEMED TO DO OKAY DURING THE YEAR HE WAS MISSING, PA. IN FACT, GUYS LIKE LUTHOR ACTUALLY BLOOMED.

BUT WHAT WAS IT LIKE MEETING JOR-EL AND LARA, SON? I KNOW THEY WEREN'T THE GENUINE ARTICLE, BUT STILL...

SEEING THEM IN THE FLESH ISN'T SOMETHING I'M GOING TO FORGET, MA, BUT IT MADE ME REALIZE SOMETHING ELSE, TOO.

JOR-EL AND LARA MIGHT HAVE BEEN MY MOTHER AND FATHER...

...BUT YOU'LL ALWAYS BE MY MA AND PA.

DEDICATED TO THE MEMORY OF JAMES AND ALICE MILLAR

END

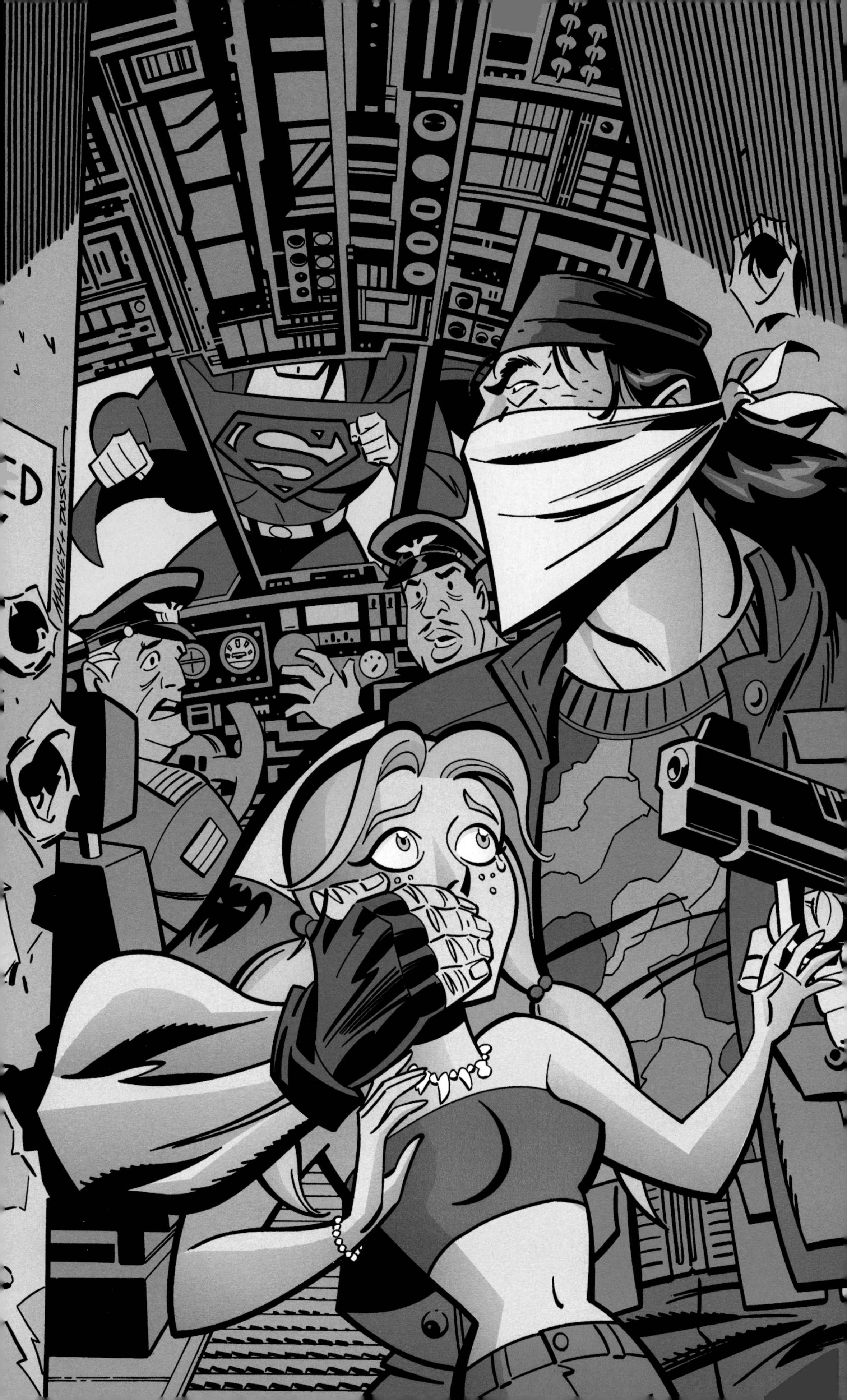

THIS IS A JOB FOR SUPERMAN

"HEY, SUPERMAN..."

CIR
METROPOL

MARK MILLAR
WRITER
ALUIR AMANCIO
PENCILLER
TERRY AUSTIN
INKER
MARIE SEVERIN
COLORIST
ZYLONOL
SEPARATIONS
PHIL FELIX
LETTERER
FRANK BERRIOS
ASSISTANT ED.
MIKE McAVENNIE
EDITOR

SUPERMAN CREATED
BY JERRY SIEGEL
AND JOE SHUSTER

...I KNOW IT'S A LONG SHOT, BUT I THOUGHT, SEEIN' AS YOU GOT SUPER-EARS, YOU MIGHT BE ABLE TO HEAR WHAT I'M SAYIN' AND HELP ME OUT WITH SOMETHIN'.

Y'SEE, MY DOG...PATCH...WENT MISSIN' A COUPLE OF DAYS AGO, WHEN WE WERE PLAYIN' IN THE PARK.

I'VE KINDA GIVEN UP ON POP FINDIN' HIM, SO I WONDERED IF YOU COULD TRACK HIM DOWN.

IT'S COOL IF YOU'RE TOO BUSY. NO HARD FEELINGS OR ANYTHING...

...BUT I'LL LEAVE THE WINDOW OPEN TONIGHT, ANYWAY, JUST IN CASE...

IS HE STILL BROKEN UP ABOUT PATCH?

WORSE THAN EVER, HONEY. THE POOR KID'S IN THERE ASKING SUPERMAN TO FIND HIM NOW.

IT'S HORRIBLE SEEING HIM DEPRESSED LIKE THIS. HE'S HARDLY TOUCHED HIS FOOD SINCE THAT DOG DISAPPEARED.

WELL, HE'S GONNA HAVE TO ACCEPT IT. AS FAR AS I CAN SEE, PATCH IS GONE FOR GOOD. THE BOY NEEDS TO GET A GRIP...

...SUPERMAN'S GOT MORE IMPORTANT THINGS TO DO WITH HIS TIME THAN LOOK FOR LITTLE LOST DOGS.

LASAGNE? BUT YOU KNOW I'M ALLERGIC TO TOMATO SAUCE!

MOMMY, WILL YOU READ ME A STORY?

DARLING, HAVE YOU SEEN MY GLASSES?

ACTUALLY, THIS IS ONE OF MY LESS EXPENSIVE SUITS...

...GOTTA READ THIS BOOK BEFORE TOMORROW'S MEETING...

TAXI!

HELP! SOMEBODY CALL THE POLICE!

STUPID GUARDS--IT'S NOT LIKE THE BANK WOULD HELP IF WE STOLE *YOUR* MONEY-- WHY SHOULD YOU CARE ABOUT *THEIRS*?

FRZZAK!

SAVE THE SOCIOLOGY DEBATE FOR *HAWAII*. WE'VE GOT ABOUT NINETY SECONDS BEFORE THE COPS GET...

DIDN'T YOU READ THE *SMALL PRINT*, BOYS? NO UNAUTHORIZED TRANSACTIONS OUTSIDE REGULAR BANKING HOURS.

WHUMMF!

WHO PAID FOR YOUR FANCY ICE-GUNS? SURELY *INTERGANG* ISN'T *DESPERATE* ENOUGH TO HIRE LOW-GRADE AMATEURS.

DON'T *UNDERESTIMATE* US, SUPERMAN!

ONE STEP CLOSER, AND WE'LL--

WHOOSH!

LET ME *GUESS*--"YOU'LL PUT ME ON *ICE*"?

WHOA!

238

WAM!

WEEOOWEEOOWEEOO

LOOK OUT, YOU CRAZY...!

HEY, FELLA-- YOU JUST RAN AN AMBULANCE OFF THE ROAD!

MISSING DOG

SUPERMAN JUST TOOK OUT THE TRASH AT THE FIRST NATIONAL BANK, BOYS AND GIRLS, BUT WE STILL HAVE A STRAY ON THE LOOSE...

...LAST SEEN HEADING ALONG EAST FOURTEENTH AND BROADWAY.

SCREECH!

WHUMP!

HOLY COW!

YEAH! AND IF YOU DON'T SHADDAP, YOU'RE GONNA NEED AN AMBULANCE!

TEN-FOUR, SARGE. CAN YOU OFFER A DESCRIPTION?

SUSPECT IS ABOUT SIX-FOOT-TWO, DRESSED IN THERMALS AND GOGGLES, AND MOST LIKELY CARRYING A FREEZE-GUN.

UM... I THINK WE'VE GOT HIM, SARGE.

239

GEEZ, WHAT A *MESS!* I GOT PLENTY OF SPACE IN MY CAB IF YOU GUYS NEED A RIDE TO THE HOSPITAL OR ANYTHING.

THANKS, PAL, BUT TRAFFIC'S BACKED UP, AND THERE'S A PREGNANT LADY IN THE BACK ABOUT TEN DEEP BREATHS AWAY FROM BEING A *MOM.*

ON TOP OF THAT, SHE'S SUFFERING COMPLICATIONS, SO A HOSPITAL BIRTH WOULD HAVE BEEN BEST FOR BOTH HER AND THE BABY...

...BUT IT LOOKS LIKE WE'RE GONNA HAVE TO DELIVER HERE AND HOPE FOR THE BEST.

SIR, IF YOU'D LIKE TO CLIMB INSIDE AND LOCK THE DOORS, I'LL HAVE YOU AT METROPOLIS GENERAL IN LESS THAN TWO MINUTES.

WHAT THE HECK...?

SUPERMAN!

DON'T FORGET TO FASTEN YOUR SEATBELTS.

AWRIGHT, S-MAN! WAY TO GO!

I COULD DROP YOU AT THE FRONT DOOR OR THE HELI-PAD, SIR...

HECK, WE'LL PROBABLY NEVER DO THIS AGAIN, SO LET'S SHOOT FOR THE HELI-PAD, SUPERMAN. I'LL RADIO AHEAD AND MAKE SURE THEY'RE READY FOR US.

DOCTOR, YOU'RE NOT GOING TO BELIEVE WHO JUST TOUCHED DOWN ON OUR ROOF!

WHAT... SUPERMAN'S HERE? ARE YOU SERIOUS?

"TAKE A LOOK AND SEE FOR YOURSELF."

IS... IS MY BABY OKAY?

YOUR BABY IS DOING GREAT, MA'AM... AND, IF YOU DON'T MIND MY SAYING SO, THE LITTLE TYKE LOOKS JUST LIKE YOU.

SUPERMAN!

CAN I HELP YOU, DOCTOR?

I CERTAINLY HOPE SO. MY TEAM AND I HAVE BEEN WAITING DOWNSTAIRS TO PERFORM A TRANSPLANT OPERATION...

...BUT THE DONOR HEART WE WERE EXPECTING HAS BEEN DELAYED AT CHICAGO AIRPORT FOR ALMOST SIX HOURS.

THE TRANSPLANT WON'T WORK IF YOU WAIT MUCH LONGER, SIR. DOESN'T AIR-TRAFFIC CONTROL APPRECIATE THE URGENCY?

THEY'RE NOT RESPONSIBLE FOR THE HOLDUP, MY FRIEND. FLIGHT 401 FROM CHICAGO HAS BEEN HIJACKED BY POLITICAL EXTREMISTS...

"...AND I DON'T THINK THE YOUNG GIRL ON LIFE SUPPORT IS HIGH ON THEIR LIST OF PRIORITIES."

LOOK AT THEM SWEAT OUT THERE!

IT'S FUNNY HOW MUCH THE WORLD PAYS ATTENTION ONCE YOU FIRE A FEW SHOTS, EH?

I SAY WE KILL SOME PASSENGERS AND DOUBLE OUR DEMANDS!

OH, DON'T BE SUCH A HAM. ALL YOU'RE DOING IS SCARING THE CHILDREN. JUST SHUT UP AND STICK WITH THE PLAN!

BOTH OF YOU SHUT UP AND-- WAIT A MINUTE!

THERE'S SOMETHING COMING TOWARDS US OUT THERE.

I DON'T LIKE THE LOOK OF THIS--!

KKLEEEESHH!

THE FEELING'S MUTUAL, FRIEND.

SUPERMAN?!

IDIOT! YOU DON'T UNDERSTAND...WE'RE NOT SOME COMMON THIEVES DOING THIS FOR MONEY! WE'RE POLITICAL ACTIVISTS, FIGHTING FOR A CAUSE!

242

MISTER, I STOPPED LISTENING THE MINUTE I SAW THE GUNS.

NOW PUT THE TOYS AWAY, GENTLE-MEN ...

BRAKKA BRAKKA BRAKKA

...THE NOISE FROM THOSE THINGS IS UPSETTING THE PASSENGERS.

YEOW!

ARRGH!

FFSSSHH!

THEN HERE'S SOMETHING ELSE TO DISTRACT THEM, YOU SYMPATHIZER:

ENOUGH EXPLOSIVE POWER TO PUT YOU, ME AND EVERY-ONE WITHIN A 500-FOOT RADIUS IN TOMORROW'S OBITUARIES!

TAK!

SHBOOM!

243

YOU WEREN'T KIDDING-- THAT ACTUALLY TINGLED.

H-HOW CAN YOU STAND THERE AND SCOFF AT PRINCIPLES WE'RE WILLING TO DIE FOR, YOU ARROGANT FOOL?

AREN'T YOU EVEN INTERESTED IN WHY WE TOOK UP ARMS AGAINST THE SYSTEM YOU SERVE WITH SUCH BLIND DEVOTION?

POLITICS WAS NEVER MY THING.

UNGH!

PLINK!

SUPERMAN! WE WERE SUPPOSED TO GET THIS TO METROPOLIS GENERAL HOURS AGO!

THERE'S A PATIENT WAITING FOR A NEW HEART,... AND,... AND SHE'S GOING TO DIE UNLESS...

EASY, MISS, THERE'S NOTHING TO WORRY ABOUT...

NO ONE'S GOING TO DIE.

"I PROMISE."

...SUPER-MAN? YES, HE DELIVERED THE HEART A FEW MINUTES AGO. TEENAGERS TRAPPED IN AN ABANDONED MINE-SHAFT? NO, I DON'T KNOW IF ANYONE TOLD HIM.

HE'S NOT THE KIND OF GUY WHO STOPS LONG ENOUGH TO TALK, YOU KNOW WHAT I MEAN?

244

THEY DON'T KNOW IF HE HEARD THE NEWS, CHIEF. GUESS WE'D BETTER ASSUME WE'RE HANDLING THIS RESCUE BY OURSELVES.

BLAST! THERE ARE STILL KIDS TRAPPED DOWN THAT OLD PIT!

DOES ANYONE HAVE ANY GOOD NEWS?

SORRY, BOSS. CAVE-IN'S EVEN WORSE THAN WE EXPECTED.

THE BEST DRILLS IN THE WORLD WOULD TAKE FOUR OR FIVE HOURS TO REACH THOSE KIDS, AND THEY'RE GONNA BE LONG DEAD BY THEN.

WHAT? BUT I THOUGHT WE ESTIMATED THERE WAS SIX HOURS' WORTH OF AIR IN THE CAVERN...?

"AIR AIN'T THE PROBLEM, BOSS. OUR READINGS SAY THE MINE SHAFT'S STARTING TO FLOOD."

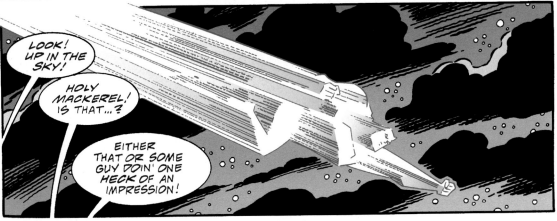

LOOK! UP IN THE SKY!

HOLY MACKEREL! IS THAT...?

EITHER THAT OR SOME GUY DOIN' ONE HECK OF AN IMPRESSION!

245

SHUDOOOM!

WHOA!

SKKTTCH RUMMBLLE

WH-WHAT'S THAT RUMBLING SOUND?

IT'S ANOTHER LANDSLIDE! WE'RE GONNA BE BURIED ALIVE!

KRKOOM!

NOT IF I HAVE ANY SAY IN THE MATTER!

SUPERMAN!

I KNEW YOU WOULDN'T LET US DOWN, BIG GUY!

YEAH! EVEN WHEN THE WATER WAS COMING UP PAST MY KNEES, ALL I WAS THINKING WAS, "WHERE'S SUPERMAN? SHOULDN'T HE BE HERE BY NOW?"

THANKS ≡hhnn≡ FOR THE VOTE OF CONFIDENCE, KIDS... BUT TWO HUNDRED FEET OF SOLID ROCK IS... HEAVIER THAN IT LOOKS...

LET'S GET... MOVING HERE, HUH?

246

GEEZ, IF I LIVE TO BE A MILLION YEARS OLD, I DON'T THINK I'LL EVER FIGURE THAT GUY OUT.

WHO, SUPERMAN? HOW D'YA MEAN?

≥ KAFF! KAFF! ≥

WELL, WE RISK OUR LIVES 'CAUSE IT'S OUR JOB, BUT HE DOES THIS STUFF PRACTICALLY 24/7 AND DOESN'T ASK FOR A NICKEL.

WHOOM!

HE SHUNS PUBLICITY, NEVER WAITS AROUND TO BE THANKED...

I MEAN, WHAT'S HIS ANGLE?

KOOM!

ATTENTION ALL UNITS! GANG FIGHT AND LOOTING IN PROGRESS ON LOWER EAST SIDE! APPROXIMATELY 12-15 TEENS, MOST OF THEM PACKING AUTOMATIC WEAPONS.

STOP WHATEVER YOU'RE DOING AND--!

≡AHEM!≡ Um, ATTENTION, UNITS. IGNORE PREVIOUS MESSAGE... SUPERMAN JUST APPEARED AND, UH, CALMED EVERYTHING DOWN.

RIOT'S OFF. OVER AND OUT.

WHAT HAPPENED HERE, OFFICER?

HMM?

OH, IT'S YOU, SUPERMAN.

WE'RE JUST WRAPPIN' UP HERE. SOME GUY TOOK A DIVE OFF THE BUILDING. LOOKS LIKE A SUICIDE.

MAN, THERE MUST BE LESS PAINFUL WAYS TO BUMP YOURSELF OFF, HUH?

duct HEAT RESISTANT

IF ONLY I COULD'VE GOT HERE A FEW MINUTES EARLIER...

AH, DON'T BEAT YOURSELF UP OVER THIS LOSER, PAL. HE'S SPENT SO MUCH TIME IN THE JOINT OVER THE YEARS, SOME OF US TALKED ABOUT GIVING HIM A KEY.

248

A HUMAN BEING JUST *DIED* HERE, OFFICER. *REGARDLESS* OF HIS PAST, THIS IS *ONE* OCCASION WHERE THE MAN DESERVES A LITTLE *RESPECT.*

CRIPES! SORRY I SPOKE...!

FORGET ABOUT *HIM,* SUPERMAN. THE GUY SHOULDA RETIRED *YEARS* AGO.

LISTEN, YOU SHOULD KNOW ABOUT THIS *NOTE* THE PARA-MEDICS JUST FOUND ON THE DECEASED.

DOES IT EXPLAIN *WHY* HE TOOK HIS OWN LIFE?

UNFORTUNATELY, IT *DOES.* APPARENTLY, OUR FRIEND HERE *MURDERED* SOMEONE AND PUT THE BLAME ON HIS *BROTHER.*

THE POOR GUY'S BEEN SENTENCED TO THE ELECTRIC CHAIR. SEEMS THE REAL KILLER WENT SIDEWALK-SWIMMING BECAUSE HE COULDN'T TAKE THE *GUILT* ANYMORE.

YOU MEAN THAT KID IN THE NEWSPAPERS IS *INNOCENT?* BUT HE'S SCHEDULED TO BE EXECUTED AT *MIDNIGHT* TONIGHT!

GOOD *LORD!* WHAT TIME IS IT *NOW?*

ELEVEN FIFTY-*NINE!* WE'D BETTER CALL STRYKER'S ISLAND...!

NO TIME! HE'LL BE *DEAD* BY THE TIME YOU GET THROUGH TO THE SWITCH-BOARD!

"BETTER LEAVE THIS TO ME."

GOD, NO... PLEASE...

CHUNNG!

SHZAAK!

KRAASH!

SUPERMAN?! THIS... THIS IS AN OUTRAGE!

WHATEVER YOUR VIEWS ON CAPITAL PUNISHMENT, THIS MAN WAS CONVICTED IN A COURT OF LAW!

EVEN YOU DON'T HAVE THE AUTHORITY TO OVERTURN A LEGAL DECISION...!

THIS POOR MAN HAS KILLED NO ONE, LADIES AND GENTLEMEN, AND I'VE GOT THE EVIDENCE IN MY HAND TO PROVE IT.

AS FOR THE REAL KILLER... WELL, HE DECIDED TO FACE HIS OWN SENTENCE TONIGHT.

THIS CASE IS CLOSED.

251

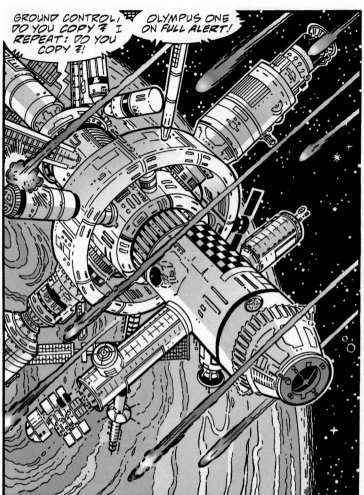

GROUND CONTROL, DO YOU COPY?! I REPEAT: DO YOU COPY?!

OLYMPUS ONE ON FULL ALERT!

IT'S NO USE! SATELLITE COM-LINK MUST BE DOWN NOW, TOO! AND THERE'S STILL NO SIGN OF THIS METEOR STORM EASING UP!

THE STATION WASN'T DESIGNED TO SUSTAIN THIS KIND OF PHYSICAL DAMAGE! WHAT ARE WE GOING TO DO?

IT MAY NOT MATTER MUCH NOW--

--THAT LAST PIECE OF SPACE DEBRIS JUST TORE A HOLE THROUGH ONE OF OUR MAIN AIR CYLINDERS!

WHAT?!

AT THE RATE WE'RE LOSING PRESSURE, I'D ESTIMATE WE ONLY HAVE ANOTHER TEN MINUTES OF OXYGEN.

OH GOD, WE'RE ACTUALLY GOING TO DIE IN SOME FREAK METEOR STORM...!

WAIT! D-DO YOU SEE THAT?

252

IT'S SUPERMAN!

THE COMPUTERS-- THEY'RE BOOTING BACK UP! WE SEEM TO HAVE POWER AGAIN!

H-HE'S GOING TO GET US *THROUGH* THIS! WE'RE GOING TO MAKE IT!

OH, NO...

"...LOOK!"

"I...I DON'T THINK HE EVEN SEES IT YET...!"

"EVEN IF HE *DID*, WHAT'S HE GOING TO *DO*? THAT THING MUST BE THE SIZE OF A SMALL *BUILDING*! HE'S..."

253

"...HE'S CHARGING RIGHT FOR IT ?!"

"HE'S CRAZY! THERE'S NO WAY EVEN HE CAN MOVE THAT AWAY FROM ..."

...US...?

HE...HE DID IT!

LOOK AT THAT! ONE PUNCH... AND HE SHATTERED THE WHOLE ROCK INTO A BILLION PIECES! UN-BELIEVABLE!

IS HE ALL RIGHT?

I THINK SO. IN FACT, I'D ALMOST SAY HE WAS SMILING.

WAY TO GO, SUPERMAN!

WOW!

OUR MORNING UPDATE BEGINS WITH SUPER-MAN'S *SENSATIONAL* SPACE RESCUE...

BOTH MOTHER AND BABY ARE FINE AFTER SUPER-MAN...

A WRONGLY-CONVICTED MAN FACING STATE EXECUTION WAS RELEASED TO TEARS OF JOY...

MORNING, BILL. DO ANYTHING INTERESTING LAST NIGHT?

...DETAILS OF THE FAILED HIJACKING IN A SPECIAL 7:30 REPORT...

FIRE CREWS WATCHED IN *AWE* AS THE MAN OF STEEL...

LAST NIGHT? NAH...

STR-RAKKK!

... MY TUESDAY NIGHTS ARE USUALLY PRETTY *QUIET.*

7:45 UPDATE...

...STOPPING A FULL-SCALE GANG WAR ONLY *MINUTES* AFTER IT BEGAN...

...BEFORE TURNING HIS ATTENTION TO THE BANK ROBBERS...

...WHAT COULD EASILY HAVE LED TO *TRAGEDY* IF NOT FOR SUPERMAN.

...GO LIVE NOW TO *METROP-OLIS GENERAL*, WHERE THE PATIENT IS RECOVERING NICELY FROM HER SUCCESSFUL TRANSPLANT...

IT'S 8:00 A.M. AND A *BEAUTIFUL* DAY IN METROP-OLIS...

SLURP!
Hhn...?

PATCH...? MOM! DAD! COME QUICK!

WHAT IS IT, SON? WHAT'S...?

IT'S PATCH! HE'S BACK! HE'S BACK!!

I LEFT THE WINDOW OPEN FOR HIM LAST NIGHT, AND SUPERMAN MUST'A BRUNG HIM HOME!

NAH... IT CAN'T BE...

I'M GLAD PATCH CAME HOME, KIDDO, BUT SUPERMAN'S BEEN ALL OVER THE NEWS THIS MORNING. HOW COULD A GUY LIKE HIM FIND THE TIME TO TRACK DOWN A MISSING DOG WHEN HE WAS SAVING PRACTICALLY THE WHOLE WORLD LAST NIGHT?

DON'TCHA GET IT, DAD...?

"...HE'S SUPERMAN!"

END

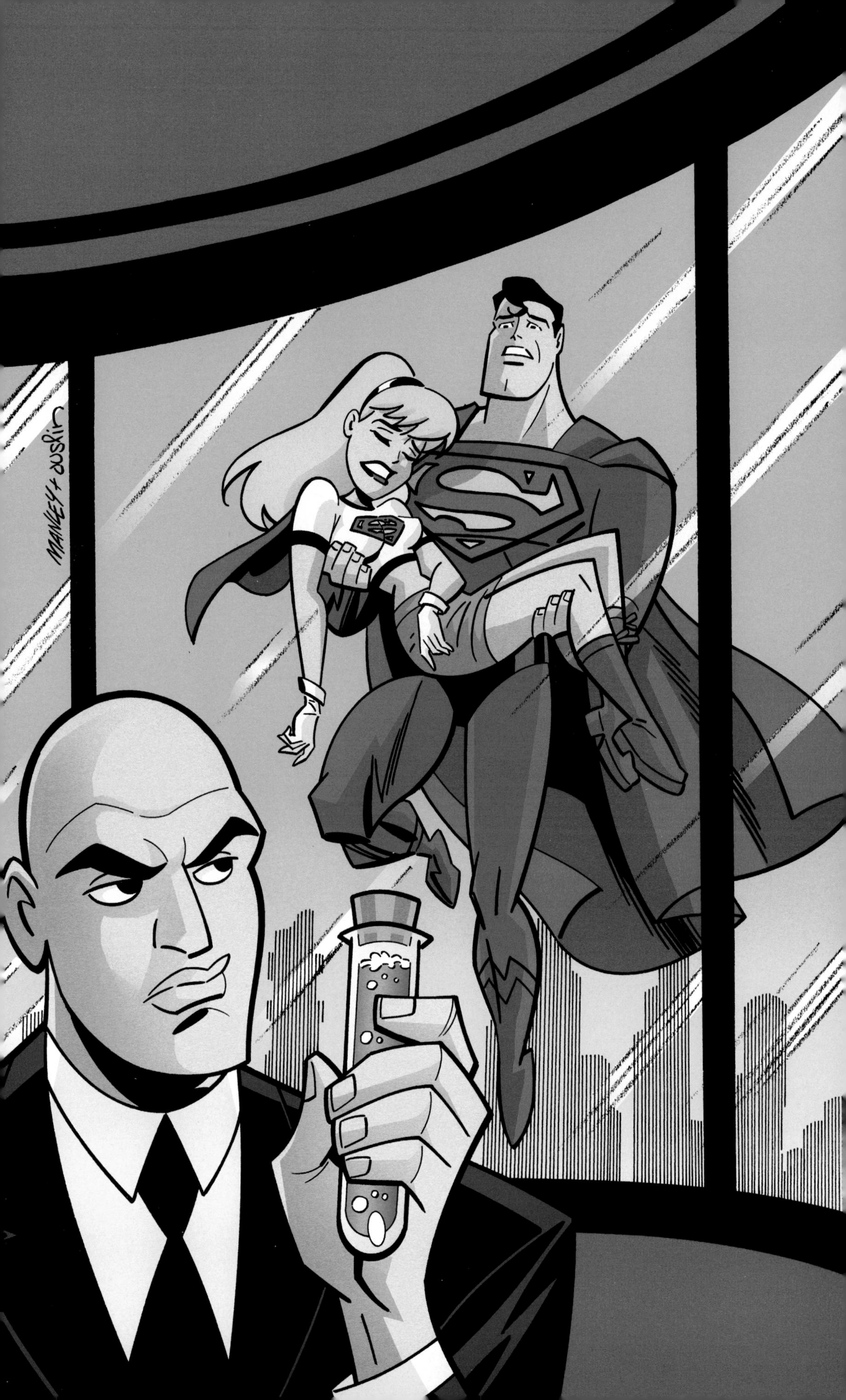
MANLEY + AUSKIN

"A DEATH IN THE FAMILY"

MARK MILLAR
STORY

ALLIR AMANCIO
PENCILLER

TERRY AUSTIN
INKER

PHIL FELIX
LETTERER

MARIE SEVERIN
COLORIST

ZYLONOL
SEPARATOR

JOEY CAVALIERI
EDITOR

SMALLVILLE...

KARA!

SUPERMAN CREATED BY JERRY SIEGEL & JOE SHUSTER

JONATHAN! GET A DOCTOR... QUICKLY! SHE'S BLACKING OUT!

THERE'S NO POINT, MARTHA.

A REGULAR DOCTOR WON'T BE ABLE TO TREAT A GIRL FROM ANOTHER PLANET...

"...CLARK'S THE ONLY ONE WHO CAN HELP HER NOW."

SOME KIND OF WEIRD FEVER?! LISTEN, PA...STAY WHERE YOU ARE AND DON'T PANIC. I CAN BE IN SMALLVILLE IN FIVE MINUTES.

HEY! ANYBODY SEEN KENT?

SHHH

GEEZ, TURN YOUR BACK FOR A SECOND AND HE'S PROBABLY SNEAKING OFF TO INVESTIGATE HIS NEXT PULITZER PRIZE-WINNING SCOOP.

HOW IS SHE, PA?

NOT GOOD, SON... AND GETTING WORSE BY THE SECOND.

I'VE SEEN A LOT OF STRANGE THINGS OVER THE YEARS, BUT NOTHING LIKE THIS. THE BLOTCHES ON HER SKIN MAKE ME WONDER IF THIS IS SOME KIND OF ALIEN VIRUS SHE'S CONTRACTED.

I FEEL SO ASHAMED. YOUR MOTHER AND I PROMISED WE'D TAKE CARE OF SUPERGIRL WHEN YOU BROUGHT HER TO THIS WORLD AND...

THIS ISN'T YOUR FAULT, PA. NO MATTER WHAT'S HAPPENED TO KARA, YOU AND MA HAVEN'T LET ANYONE DOWN.

LET'S ASSESS THE SITUATION BEFORE WE...

SHE'S STOPPED BREATHING, JONATHAN! OH, MY LORD...

I THINK KARA'S DEAD.

NO, MY SUPER-HEARING'S JUST PICKED UP A HEARTBEAT. IT'S SLOW AND IRREGULAR, BUT SHE'S DEFINITELY ALIVE... FOR THE MOMENT.

BUM-BUMP!

261

DO SOMETHING, CLARK. USE YOUR POWERS AND MAKE EVERYTHING RIGHT AGAIN.

YOU KNOW IT ISN'T THAT SIMPLE, MA, I'M HARDLY AN EXPERT IN HUMAN PHYSIOLOGY AND UNDERSTAND VIRTUALLY NOTHING ABOUT WHAT MAKES AN ARGOAN LIKE KARA TICK, BUT...

YES?

PA'S GUESS WAS RIGHT ABOUT THE VIRUS BEING ALIEN IN ORIGIN. I CAN SEE TRACES OF AN UNFAMILIAR TOXIN IN HER BLOODSTREAM.

IT'S A VIRAL INFECTION, ALL RIGHT, AND IT'S ATTACKING EVERY PART OF HER BODY INCLUDING THE BRAIN... WHICH EXPLAINS THE COMA STATE.

BUT HOW COULD SHE CATCH SOMETHING LIKE THIS?

THAT'S RIGHT. WE TOLD HER SHE'D BE GROUNDED FOR A MONTH IF SHE SO MUCH AS SET FOOT IN OUTER SPACE AGAIN AFTER LAST TIME.

I DON'T KNOW, MA, BUT SHE NEEDS URGENT ATTENTION!

LET'S HOPE THE EQUIPMENT AT MY FORTRESS OF SOLITUDE CAN GIVE US SOME ANSWERS BEFORE IT'S TOO LATE.

I'M NOT SURE IF YOU CAN HEAR ME IN THERE, KARA...

...BUT I WANT YOU TO KNOW EVERYTHING'S GOING TO BE FINE, REGARDLESS OF HOW BAD THINGS LOOK RIGHT NOW.

MY SUSPICION IS THAT THIS INFECTION IS NATIVE TO YOUR HOME-WORLD OF ARGO... MEANING THE RELEVANT DETAILS SHOULD BE STORED ON BRAINIAC'S KRYPTONIAN INFORMATION ORB.

ONCE DIAGNOSED, THE COMPUTER SHOULD BE ABLE TO GIVE US THE FORMULA FOR AN ANTIDOTE...

...IN THEORY, AT LEAST.

ARE YOU READY?

263

GREETINGS, KAL-EL. HOW MAY I BE OF ASSISTANCE?

ACCESS FILES ON THE PLANET ARGO, BRAINIAC.

ARGO: FOURTH WORLD IN ORBIT AROUND OUR KRYPTONIAN RED SUN.

POPULATION: TEN BILLION. PREDOMINANT SPECIES: HUMANOID. PREDOMINANT RELIGION: RAOISM. CAPITAL: ARGO CITY.

ARGO

ART/LITERATURE
SCIENCE/MEDICINE
HISTORY
SPORTING

GEOGRA
POLITI
COM
TE

KRYPTON

DO YOU WISH TO CONTINUE?

SELECT "SCIENCE AND MEDICINE" AND ACCESS "VIRTUAL CLINIC."

VIRTUAL CLINIC OPERATIONAL.

BEGIN HEMATOLOGICAL EXAMINATION OF KARA IN-ZE, NATIVE OF ARGO, AND DISPLAY DIAGNOSIS IN THREE-DIMENSIONAL IMAGES.

THE FEMALE IS SUFFERING FROM A VIRAL INFECTION DERIVED FROM NATURALLY-OCCURRING BACTERIA KNOWN AS ENCYOPYLAS TRANSLOCI...

...PICTURED HERE IN ITS MOST BASIC FORM.

THE VIRUS WAS THE MOST FEARED KILLER ON ARGO, PERIODICALLY WIPING OUT GREAT SECTIONS OF THE POPULATION UNTIL A CURE WAS DISCOVERED BY VAR-EL OF KRYPTON...

BUT WHAT APPEARED TO BE AN INSURMOUNTABLE MEDICAL PROBLEM WAS ALMOST ENTIRELY ELIMINATED...

...BY THE INOCULATION OF EVERY NATIVE ARGOAN CHILD WHEN HE OR SHE REACHED THE AGE OF FIFTEEN.

THE SUCCESS RATE WAS 99.92%.

IS THIS WHY KARA DEVELOPED THE VIRUS? BECAUSE SHE WASN'T OLD ENOUGH TO BE INOCULATED WHEN ARGO WAS DESTROYED?

AFFIRMATIVE.

IS THE FORMULA FOR VAR-EL'S ANTIDOTE STILL ON FILE?

AFFIRMATIVE.

TERRIFIC! PREPARE A LIST OF INGREDIENTS AND LET'S GET THIS YOUNG LADY BACK ON HER FEET, BRAINIAC.

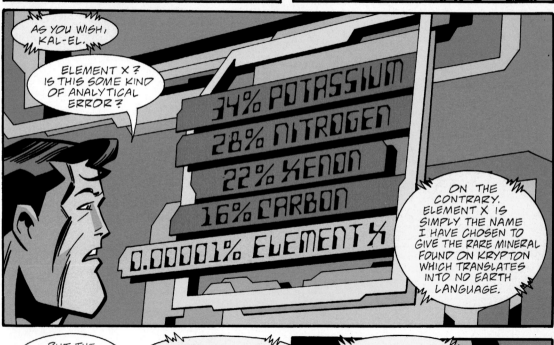

AS YOU WISH, KAL-EL.

ELEMENT X? IS THIS SOME KIND OF ANALYTICAL ERROR?

34% POTASSIUM
28% NITROGEN
22% XENON
16% CARBON
0.00001% ELEMENT X

ON THE CONTRARY. ELEMENT X IS SIMPLY THE NAME I HAVE CHOSEN TO GIVE THE RARE MINERAL FOUND ON KRYPTON WHICH TRANSLATES INTO NO EARTH LANGUAGE.

BUT THE ELEMENT CAN BE FOUND HERE, RIGHT?

UNFORTUNATELY NOT, KAL-EL. KRYPTON'S PERIODIC TABLE CONTAINED FOUR METALS AND AN INERT GAS EXCLUSIVE TO YOUR BIRTH-WORLD.

ELEMENT X DOES NOT NATURALLY EXIST ON PLANET EARTH.

I'M AFRAID THIS ONE HAS US BEAT, SUPERMAN...

...EVEN FOLLOWING THE SUBMOLECULAR IMAGES YOU GAVE US, WE CAN BARELY COMPREHEND ELEMENT X LET ALONE DUPLICATE IT.

ITS ATOMIC STRUCTURE IS UNLIKE ANYTHING WE'VE EVER SEEN.

THERE MUST BE SOMETHING YOU CAN DO, PROFESSOR...

...I REFUSE TO ACCEPT THE NOTION OF A NO-WIN SCENARIO!

MAYBE DUPLICATION IS THE WRONG APPROACH. COULDN'T YOU JUST FLY TO ARGO AND BRING BACK FRESH SUPPLIES OF THE FORMULA?

"I REALIZE KRYPTON'S EXPLOSION DISLODGED THE PLANET FROM ITS ORBIT AND THE WHOLE PLACE IS COVERED IN A SHROUD OF ICE...

"...BUT IF THIS VIRUS WAS AS WIDE-SPREAD AS YOU SAY, YOU SHOULD BE ABLE TO FIND TRACES OF THE ANTIDOTE SOMEWHERE."

NOT EVEN AN OPTION, PROFESSOR.

EARTH TO ARGO, EVEN AT FULL SPEED, WOULD TAKE A COUPLE OF DAYS, AND, ACCORDING TO BRAINIAC, SUPERGIRL IS IN THE ADVANCED STAGES OF THIS VIRUS...

I'M AFRAID IF WE CAN'T FIND OR DUPLICATE ELEMENT X HERE, SUPERGIRL WILL BE DEAD IN TWENTY-FOUR HOURS.

GOOD LORD... THIS JUST GETS WORSE BY THE SECOND.

YOU'RE ALL EXPERTS IN YOUR FIELD... BRILLIANT MEN AND WOMEN WITH IMPECCABLE CREDENTIALS.

DOESN'T ANYONE EVEN HAVE A SUGGESTION TO MAKE?

WHY DON'T YOU ASK LEX LUTHOR?

EXCUSE ME?

HE'S THE SMARTEST MAN IN METROPOLIS, RIGHT?

AND TO WHAT DO I OWE THE PLEASURE?

I NEED YOUR HELP, LUTHOR.

DOING ANYTHING TONIGHT, MERCY?

YEAH, DUMPING YOUR BODY IN THE EAST RIVER AND INVENTING AN ALIBI UNLESS YOU GET OUT OF MY FACE, DOG-BREATH.

F-FORGET I EVEN ASKED.

DEET!

MISS GRAVES?

WHAT'S UP, BOSS?

CANCEL EVERY APPOINTMENT FOR THE NEXT TWENTY-FOUR HOURS AND MAKE SURE MY PRIVATE LABORATORY IS FULLY FUNCTIONAL.

FLASH OF INSPIRATION TO MAKE ANOTHER BILLION DOLLARS, LEX?

SOMETHING EVEN MORE VALUABLE, MERCY...

...I PLAN TO SAVE A GIRL'S LIFE.

270

YOU NEVER CEASE TO SURPRISE ME, LUTHOR.

WHY? BECAUSE YOU ASSUME, IN YOUR ARROGANT WAY, THAT YOU'RE THE ONLY ONE CAPABLE OF DOING GOOD IN METROPOLIS, SUPERMAN?

I MIGHT DESPISE THE EMBLEM THIS CHILD CHOOSES TO WEAR ON HER CHEST, BUT THE TRUTH IS THAT SHE'S IRRELEVANT TO OUR FEUD...

"...AND BESIDES, YOU KNOW I CAN'T RESIST A STIMULATING, CEREBRAL CHALLENGE."

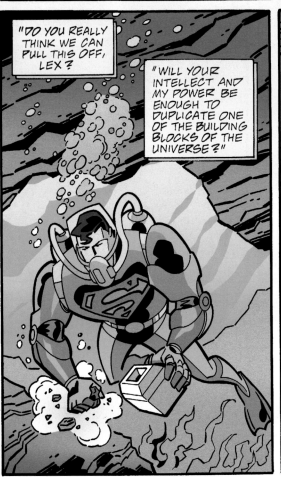

"DO YOU REALLY THINK WE CAN PULL THIS OFF, LEX?"

"WILL YOUR INTELLECT AND MY POWER BE ENOUGH TO DUPLICATE ONE OF THE BUILDING BLOCKS OF THE UNIVERSE?"

FAILURE IS INCONCEIVABLE, SUPERMAN...

...IF NATURE CAN CREATE THIS ELEMENT OUT OF NOTHING, THEN BY ALL THAT'S HOLY, SO CAN LEX LUTHOR!

271

WOULD THE EXPRESSION "EUREKA" BE TOO CONTRIVED?

ARE YOU SERIOUS? YOU'VE CREATED ELEMENT X?

DON'T LOOK SO SURPRISED. I LIKE TO LIVE UP TO MY REPUTATION AS A GENIUS EVERY ONCE IN A WHILE.

SUPERGIRL STILL HAS TWO HOURS TO SPARE WHICH SHOULD BE PLENTY OF TIME FOR YOU, WITH YOUR GREAT SPEED, TO COMPLETE THE REST OF VAR-EL'S FORMULA AND BRING HER BACK FROM THE EDGE...

...OR, AT LEAST, IT WOULD BE IF I PLANNED TO GIVE IT TO YOU.

WHAT?

GOTCHA.

LUTHOR, PLEASE. TELL ME YOU'RE JOKING...

OH, BUT I'M DEADLY SERIOUS, SUPERMAN, AND THE SIGHT OF YOUR HOPES BEING CRUSHED IS EVERY BIT AS DELICIOUS AS I HAD ANTICIPATED.

I'M NOT SURE WHAT DELIGHTS ME MOST... THE IDEA THAT MY TIME-WASTING TACTICS LEAVE YOU NO HOPE OF FINDING ANOTHER SOLUTION...

...OR THE NOTION THAT YOUR WORST ENEMY IS THE ONE MAN WHO CAN SAVE HER.

EITHER WAY, THIS "SUPER-GIRL" DIES TONIGHT!

YOU TREACHEROUS SLIME!

CAREFUL, ALIEN. THIS WHOLE EXCHANGE IS BEING VIDEO-TAPED, AND A SENATOR WOULD BE CHEAPER TO REPLACE THAN THIS JAPANESE SUIT MY PEOPLE HAD IMPORTED THIS MORNING.

YOU'RE A MONSTER...

AND WHAT KIND OF IDIOT COMES TO A MONSTER FOR HELP?

THE FORTRESS OF SOLITUDE...

HOW MUCH LONGER DOES KARA HAVE LEFT, COMPUTER?

ONLY FIFTY-NINE MINUTES, SUPERMAN. HOPE IS FADING FAST THAT S.T.A.R. LABS WILL FIND A SOLUTION IN TIME.

WRONG. THERE'S ALWAYS HOPE.

DEET!

THE MAN OF STEEL! WHAT A PLEASANT SURPRISE!

NO MORE GAMES, LUTHOR. THIS IS BIGGER THAN JUST YOU AND ME. A LIFE IS AT STAKE HERE AND I'M BEGGING YOU FOR HELP NOW.

YOU'VE GOT ME EXACTLY WHERE YOU'VE ALWAYS WANTED ME... JUST NAME YOUR PRICE.

YOU'LL DO ANYTHING I COMMAND IN EXCHANGE FOR ELEMENT X?

ANYTHING.

274

WELL, SUPERMAN, IF YOU'D DISPLAYED SUCH AN AGREEABLE ATTITUDE WHEN WE FIRST MET I DO BELIEVE WE COULD HAVE BEEN FRIENDS.

HOWEVER, LEX LUTHOR IS NOTHING IF NOT A FORGIVING SOUL AND A TACTICIAN PAR EXCELLENCE...

"THIS SCENARIO WAS ANTICIPATED, OF COURSE, AND THE TRUTH IS THAT THERE IS SOMETHING I'D LIKE YOU TO DO FOR ME..."

"I WANT YOU TO BREAK INTO STRYKER'S ISLAND PENITENTIARY..."

"LOCATE WHATEVER BUNKER THEY'RE HIDING METALLO INSIDE..."

"...PRY OPEN HIS LEAD-BASED CHEST PLATE..."

"...AND EXPOSE YOURSELF TO A FATAL DOSE OF KRYPTONITE RADIATION."

BASICALLY, THE ONLY CIRCUMSTANCES UNDER WHICH I'LL PROVIDE AN ANTIDOTE FOR THE GIRL IS IF YOU TAKE YOUR OWN LIFE, MY FRIEND.

ARE YOU READY TO PAY THE ULTIMATE PRICE FOR THE SECRET OF ELEMENT X?

LIKE I ALREADY SAID, LUTHOR...

275

"...WHATEVER IT TAKES."

SUPERMAN, I... I'M SURE I SPEAK FOR ALL OF US WHEN I SAY...

PLEASE, PROFESSOR. NO TEARS.

I'M ONLY CHOKED UP BECAUSE, AFTER FORTY-EIGHT HOURS OF UNCERTAINTY, I KNOW FOR A FACT THAT SUPERGIRL IS GOING TO LIVE AND WE'RE NO LONGER FACING MILLION-TO-ONE ODDS.

BUT WHAT KIND OF GHOUL WOULD ASK YOU TO KILL YOURSELF?

I'M AFRAID THE DEAL DEPENDS ON THE IDENTITY OF OUR MYSTERIOUS BENEFACTOR REMAINING A SECRET, PROFESSOR.

ALL I CAN SAY IS GOODBYE AND THANKS FOR ALL THE HARD WORK.

WE'LL NEVER FORGET YOU, SUPERMAN.

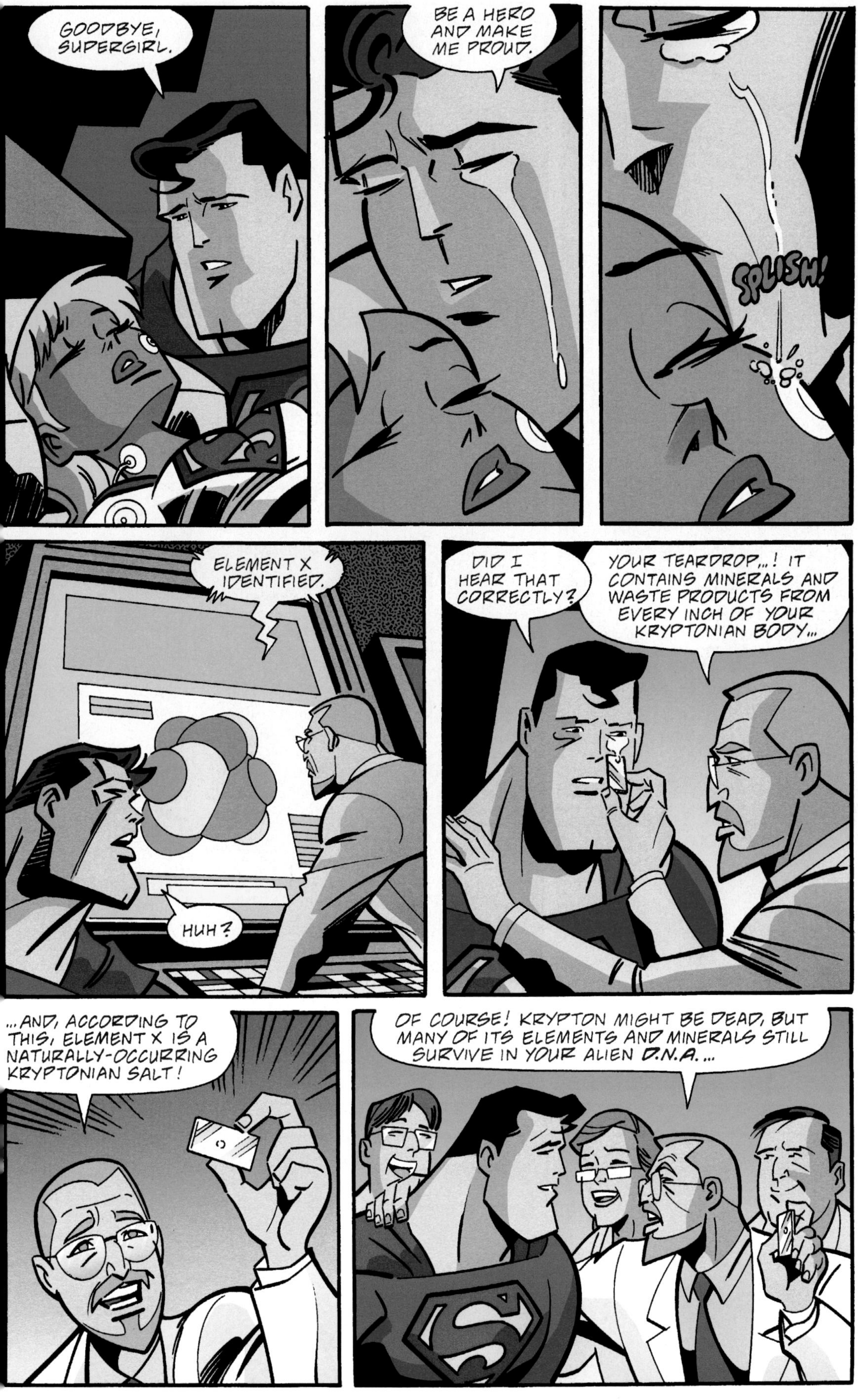
GOODBYE, SUPERGIRL.
BE A HERO AND MAKE ME PROUD.
SPLISH!
ELEMENT X IDENTIFIED.
HUH?
DID I HEAR THAT CORRECTLY?
YOUR TEARDROP...! IT CONTAINS MINERALS AND WASTE PRODUCTS FROM EVERY INCH OF YOUR KRYPTONIAN BODY...
...AND, ACCORDING TO THIS, ELEMENT X IS A NATURALLY-OCCURRING KRYPTONIAN SALT!
OF COURSE! KRYPTON MIGHT BE DEAD, BUT MANY OF ITS ELEMENTS AND MINERALS STILL SURVIVE IN YOUR ALIEN D.N.A. ...

"YOU'VE BEEN CARRYING ELEMENT X AROUND ALL THE TIME!"

OH, NO...

SEE YOU AROUND, BALDY.

NOOO OOO!

WHAT'S THE PROBLEM, BOSS?

HE SAVED HER! SUPERMAN CREATED AN EXTINCT ELEMENT OUT OF NOTHING AND SAVED SUPERGIRL'S LIFE! HE BEAT ME!

YEAH, WELL...WE'LL JUST BOUNCE BACK WITH A BIGGER AND BETTER PLAN, LEX. THAT'S THE WAY THE GAME WORKS, RIGHT?

YOU DON'T UNDERSTAND, MERCY...

I WAS LYING WHEN I TOLD HIM I'D RECREATED ELEMENT X.

THE WHOLE THING WAS A RUSE TO BRING HIM UNDER MY CONTROL, BUT HE ACTUALLY SUCCEEDED WHERE LEX LUTHOR FAILED.

SUPERMAN HAS BEATEN ME INTELLECTUALLY.

BOSS, I... I DUNNO WHAT TO SAY.

279

DON'T SAY ANYTHING, MERCY, JUST GO...

LEAVE ME ALONE WITH MY THOUGHTS.

THE END